LOOPER
PEDAL GUITAR LESSONS

BY CHAD JOHNSON

ISBN 978-1-5400-8095-0

HAL•LEONARD®

Visit Hal Leonard Online at
www.halleonard.com

World headquarters, contact:
Hal Leonard
7777 West Bluemound Road
Milwaukee, WI 53213
Email: info@halleonard.com

In Europe, contact:
Hal Leonard Europe Limited
42 Wigmore Street
Marylebone, London, W1U 2RN
Email: info@halleonardeurope.com

In Australia, contact:
Hal Leonard Australia Pty. Ltd.
4 Lentara Court
Cheltenham, Victoria, 3192 Australia
Email: info@halleonard.com.au

Contents

Introduction

Welcome to *Looper Pedal Guitar Lessons*! In this book/video, we're going to dive deep into the exciting world of looping. Over the past decade, looping has exploded in popularity, with countless players exploiting the newest technology to truly become "one-man (or one-woman!) bands." From the mostly guitar-based looping of Ed Sheeran, to the vocal-heavy layering of Reggie Watts or the multi-instrument sonic walls of sound from Jacob Collier, artists of disparate genres are turning the looping concept into an art form unto itself.

Although we'll mostly be dealing with guitar in this method, we'll also cover some additional concepts that will be very handy to the singer/songwriters among us as well. Whether you're just getting interested in the idea and haven't even purchased a looper yet, or you've fully caught the looping bug and are looking for some new ideas get the most out of your setup, you're in the right place.

Some of the many topics we'll cover include:

- Equipment—including different types of loop pedals and how to set up a live or studio looping rig

- How a looper pedal works and what types of features are available

- How to choose the best looper pedal for your needs

- Basic techniques with a single-loop pedal

- Advanced techniques possible with multi-track loopers

- Using other effect pedals in conjunction with the looper

- How to incorporate a mic looper to expand your possibilities further

Though it's hard to define the exact origin of looping—it was originally performed by the use of tape machines—looping technology has certainly come a long way since the 1950s. The feature set of modern loopers is inspiring, to say the least, and it's easy to lose yourself in hours of fun the first time you take the plunge. And that's the aim of this book: to have fun exploring these awesome machines. I hope you enjoy the journey as much as I have!

How to Use This Book

This book begins with the assumption that you know practically next to nothing about loopers (or looping in general). We'll progress in complexity throughout, so it's important to understand the fundamentals before tackling the more advanced chapters. Therefore, if you're already familiar with the basics of looping, I'd suggest at least skimming through the first few chapters to make sure you're familiar with the terminology and conventions used in this book.

If you're brand new to the subject and haven't purchased a looper yet, be sure to check out Chapter 1 before you do. We'll talk about the various features available and help determine which type of looper will best suit your specific needs. This way, you won't end up spending extra money on features you're not going to use. Or, if you already own a basic looper and are looking to step up to a more sophisticated model, you'll find the information you need in Chapter 1 to make an informed decision on that as well.

Nearly all of my looping demonstrations are notated here (and performed on the accompanying video) for you to see. This way, you'll know exactly what's going on, even as the loops get a bit more complex. Of course, you'll soon want to start creating your own loops, but at the very least, the examples shown in this book can be used as practice material while learning the ins and outs of your particular unit.

Notational Conventions

Although digital looping has been around for well over a decade, it's still a relatively new kid on the block regarding how it's notated on paper. In this book, we'll use the following terms and conventions to indicate how the various loops are used and controlled.

Start Loop

This direction instructs you to start recording a loop. For example, if you're laying down the first riff to be looped in a song, this direction will appear as "Start Loop 1." If you have a multi-track looper—i.e., able to store more than one loop—you may see this direction given for various loops ("Start Loop 2," etc.).

End Loop

This is usually the second direction you'll see, and it tells you when to stop recording the loop. Once you do this, the loop should start playing back from the beginning. So after seeing "Start Loop 1," for example, you'd see this description as "End Loop 1."

Overdub on Loop

This tells you to start recording an overdub on top of your loop. In other words, if Loop 1 consists of a bass line, you may overdub some chords on top of it, or vice versa. If more than one loop is present, this direction will specify the loop number—i.e., "Overdub on Loop 1."

End Overdub

This tells you when to stop recording your overdub. The direction will usually coincide with the end of the looped phrase, but this is only because you'll usually be playing something right up until that point. If you only need to overdub a few notes in the middle of the loop, for example, there's no reason you couldn't stop overdubbing immediately after the last note.

w/ Loop (with Loop)

This direction simply tells you that the loop(s) should be playing as you're overdubbing a new loop. It's placed at the beginning of a new section of music. If multiple loops are present, the numbers will be indicated—i.e., "w/ Loop 1" or "w/ Loops 1 & 3," etc.

Loop Off

This direction tells you to turn a loop off. This could simply be because you want to thin out the texture—kill the drum beat, for example—or it may be because you need to play a part "live" (such as a new chord progression) that would clash with one or more of the loops. Again, specific loops will be indicated when necessary—i.e., "Loop 1 off" or "Loops 1 & 2 off," etc.

Loop On

If a loop has been turned off, this direction tells you to turn it back on. It will appear at the beginning of the new section where the loop returns. Note that this direction will only appear if the loop has been previously turned off. Otherwise, the "w/ Loop" direction will appear at any new section in which the loop is used.

Because a loop you set is going to be repeated immediately after you end recording, looped phrases will be surrounded by repeat signs in the music (‖: :‖). Feel free to let the loop play as long as you'd like/need before moving on.

You'll see different combinations of the above directions throughout the book, depending on the examples at hand. For example, you won't see a reference to "Loop 2" in Chapter 2 because we won't start dealing with multi-track loopers until Chapter 3. In the final chapter, however, which features two full-song performances, you're likely to see all of them.

About the Video

Throughout the book, we'll be using many different examples to illustrate the concepts in action, almost all of which will be demonstrated on the accompanying videos. All content from the book that appears in the videos will be marked with an icon (▶). You can access these videos by looking on page 1 (title page) for the box with the 16-digit code that says "ENTER CODE." Then, just go to *www.halleonard.com/mylibrary* and enter this code to stream and/or download these videos.

This is an invaluable asset and should definitely be used in conjunction with the text throughout. It's one thing to understand the concepts on paper, but it's another thing to see the process in action. Needless to say, there's a decent amount of tap-dancing when using a looper, so if you're not accustomed to using many effects pedals, it may take some getting used to. But as you'll see in the videos, it's usually very manageable with a bit of preparation.

For all the video performances, I used the following loop devices:

- TC Electronic Ditto X4 Looper
- TC Electronic Ditto Mic Looper
- TC Helicon VoiceLive 3 Extreme

Notable Artists

Be sure to check out some notable looping artists to hear how they're each approaching the topic. You'll no doubt be inspired to try some things you hadn't thought of before (or maybe didn't even know were possible!). Just as with playing an instrument, everyone has their own personal approach to looping, and even the same unit can be used in quite a different fashion from one person to the next. From simple to extremely complex, there are plenty of approaches to looping. A list of notable loop artists would be quite long indeed, but here are a few names to get you started:

Ed Sheeran

Reggie Watts

Zoe Keating

Terry Riley

Julien Baker

Tash Sultana

The PETEBOX

Kimbra

Robert Fripp

Randolf Arriola

Julia Easterlin

Jarle Bernhoft

tUnE-yArDs

Beardyman

Ricoloop

These artists cover a wide range of genres, but even if one isn't exactly your cup of tea, I encourage you to check out a few performances just to see how they're using various looping techniques to achieve their own musical vision. You may just discover a few ideas you hadn't thought of before. Most importantly, have fun exploring the world of looping!

Chapter 1: What Is a Looper?

If looping is brand new (or even relatively new) to you, this is the place to start. In this chapter, we're going to talk about the different types of loopers available, what they do, and how to go about choosing one that best suits your needs. Keep in mind that, since looping is a burgeoning trend, new developments are being made on a regular basis with regards to loop technology. Although the information contained in this chapter is up-to-date as of now, that may change rather quickly. Nevertheless, all the features and concepts described here will likely be present in any future loopers as well, so none of this information should become obsolete for quite some time.

Looping Over Time: A Brief History

When we talk about a "looper," what do we mean, exactly? Perhaps the simplest definition is a device that can record sound and then play it back indefinitely. If we accept the parameters of that definition, then we can see examples of looping dating back quite a while.

The first looping devices to be used in live performance (and in the studio) were reel-to-reel tape recorders. Normally operated with a reel of tape spooling from a supply reel to a take-up reel in one direction, a "loop" can be created by splicing one piece of tape end-to-end, which, when threaded around both reels, will play indefinitely. The speed of the tape machine can be varied to lengthen or shorten the loop—which affects the pitch as well—to a degree. In order to create longer loops, however, artists began spooling the other end of the loop around any cylindrical object (a pole, a beer bottle, a second tape machine with no reels, etc.) that's set to the proper distance to keep the loop taut.

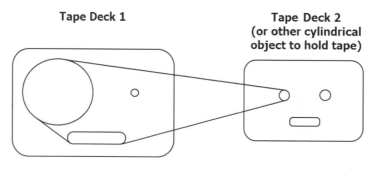

Basic tape loop

Artists such as Pierre Schaeffer and Terry Riley began implementing tape loops in the 1940s and 1950s to produce minimalist compositions and musique concrète. Minimalist Steve Reich also made use of a technique he called *phasing*, in which he would play two loops simultaneously on two tape machines set to slightly different playback speeds. This resulted in the loops drifting further and further apart after each pass (and then eventually back together). The concept found its way into popular music by the 1960s, as loops appeared in the Jamaican dub music of producers King Tubby and Sylvan Morris. Perhaps most famously, tape loops featured prominently in the Beatles' "Tomorrow Never Knows" from the *Revolver* album (1966), which made use of five loops running simultaneously.

Composers Brian Eno (of Roxy Music fame) and Robert Fripp began experimenting with tape looping in the 1970s, using a system that would eventually become known as "Frippertronics." In this system, two tape machines are used. A performance (or sequence from a synthesizer, etc.) is sent to a mixer and then on to the first machine's input. The tape from the supply reel of the first machine is then sent to the take-up reel of the second machine. The audio outputs of the second machine are then fed back into different inputs of the mixer, which is again sent to the inputs of the first machine, and so on. The effect is a continuous overdubbing of sound from one machine to the next.

With the advent of digital recording and sampling in the late 1970s and 1980s, tape looping began to fall out of fashion. The early digital delays didn't have very long times by today's standards, and most of the early designs were rack-mounted units. Legendary bass virtuoso Jaco Pastorius was one of the first to exploit this technology in a modern way with his MXR-113 digital delay (1976). Capable of 1280 ms (1.28 seconds) of delay time (after an optional upgrade), the unit also featured a footswitch-controlled "hold" function, which essentially repeated the delayed signal indefinitely, allowing sound-on-sound stacking. With this feature, Jaco would overdub several bass parts to create a short loop and then solo over the top of it (or play bass lines below it). Guitar virtuoso Eric Johnson also uses the MXR in a similar way, usually to hold a chord over which he improvises.

Subsequent digital units provided longer delay times and more features. A few standouts over the years include:

- **Arion DDS-1 and DDS-4 (1982)**: One of the earliest digital delay designs to appear in a pedal format, these units (there doesn't seem to be any difference between the two other than the name) allowed for about four seconds of delay time and, most importantly, allowed for sampling (recording). This sample could then be triggered by a remote switch and played back indefinitely. ("DDS" stands for "Digital Delay Sampler.")

- **Electro-Harmonix EH16 (1983)**: Another pedal design, this unit allowed for 16 seconds of looping, provided a metronome, and used an intuitive, bar-length feature to set the loop time. It also featured modulation effects and the ability to mix and match reverse recording with forward (normal) recording.

- **TC Electronic 2290 (1986)**: This powerful rack-mount unit allowed for 30 seconds of delay time and a host of other features, including 100 recallable presets, full MIDI control, and numerous modulation effects. It also allowed for storage/playback of 100 extensively editable samples.

- **Paradis Loop Delay (1992), Oberheim Echoplex (1994), Gibson Echoplex (2000)**: The Paradis Loop Delay, first introduced in 1992, was a powerful looping device with numerous features not shown in other similar devices. It shipped with 50 seconds of loop time but could be upgraded to nearly 200 seconds. It was succeeded by the Oberheim Echoplex and then, when Gibson bought Oberheim, the Gibson Echoplex, which eventually became the Echoplex EDP (Pro Plus). This is still an incredibly popular looper today, and it's easy to see why. It can store up to 16 loops and allows for incredibly intuitive operation, all with the feet. Although it can only play back one loop at a time, this is a hardly a limitation when you consider all the features available, including *Copy* (allows you to copy a loop to another slot), *Multiply* (doubles the length of a loop), *Replace* (drop in new audio in place of the old in a loop), *Reverse* (plays/records a loop in reverse), and more. So while it may seem that being able to play only one loop at a time is a limitation, the truth is that it's very easy to set up so many different loops of varying complexity that it's hardly an issue.

- **Line6 DL4 (1999)**: An affordable delay in a large foot pedal package, the DL4 was popular, especially in the early 2000s, and can still be found on many pedal boards today. With a 14-second loop time and several helpful features (Play Once, Half Speed/Reverse, etc.), as well as being a versatile and convincing delay modeler, this was a hit for Line6.

- **Akai Headrush (1999)**: This pedal combined an impressive tape delay emulator with a digital delay/looper capable of 23 seconds of looping time. Acoustic singer-songwriter K.T. Tunstall has made famous use of this pedal (eventually replacing it with the Headrush E2 a few years later) throughout her career, as has Radiohead's Thom Yorke (E2).

- **Boss RC-20 Loop Station (2001)**: The first loop station from Boss became a very popular looper in its day. The RC-20 allowed for a full five minutes and 30 seconds of loop time as well as several other features, including Guide Click and Loop Quantize, Realtime Tempo Change (change the tempo without affecting pitch), mic and auxiliary inputs, and 10 storable loops. Boss has continued to release numerous successful subsequent loopers in their RC line.

- **Electro-Harmonix 2880 (2005)**: Electro-Harmonix pushed the looping boundaries with the 2880, which allowed for four separate, eight-minute loops to be played back at once, each with their own faders and pan controls (for when operating in stereo). Additional controls like Reverse, Octave, and Quantize, among others, allow for additional sound-shaping. Visually, it's very intuitive as well, since it more closely resembles a 4-track recorder than a guitar pedal. This pedal was updated to the 45000 in 2013, adding even more features. Both the 2880 and 45000 have been championed by looping legend Reggie Watts, among others.

By the early to mid-2000s, we'd pretty much entered the modern era of loop stations, in which features like multi-track looping, extensive record time (several minutes or more), and numerous effects began to become commonplace among many units. But let's take a step back and examine some of these features from the ground up so we can better understand exactly what a looper does and why.

Software Loopers

It should be mentioned that many contemporary loopers make extensive use of software, such as Ableton Live, in their looping setups. This is a whole other can of worms with regard to rigs, and we won't be dealing with any software loopers in this book. We'll stick to hardware versions only, which are certainly quite popular as well.

Looper Features

There are more loopers on the market today than you can shake a stick at, and deciding on one can be quite a daunting task. If you've not yet purchased your first looper, then good for you! You'll soon be quite informed and will no doubt have a much easier time choosing one that suits your needs. In this section, we're going to take a cursory look at most of the features that you're likely to find on many of the models available. Just as a new car will come in numerous option packages, so do loopers. Do you need only the basics, every bell and whistle available, or something in between? By the end of this chapter, that choice should be clear.

The Bare Necessities

Let's first talk about basic looping features 101. These features are required in order for the unit to be properly called a looper in the first place. In other words, any looper you choose will be able to do these things.

Record and Play Back a Loop Indefinitely

Seems simple enough, right? A looper can record a loop and play it back. In other words, it can *loop*. But there's a bit more to it than that. The main variable here is *loop time*. How long can the loop be? How long do you need? Even the most basic of loopers these days will usually afford you several minutes of loop time. TC Electronic's Ditto Looper, for example, provides five minutes of loop time, while Boss' most modestly priced looper, the RC-1 Loop Station, allows for 12 minutes, both of which should be more than adequate for even the most ambitious looping artist.

TC Electronic Ditto Looper

However, there are also many multi-effect units, such as the Digitech RP360 or Zoom G3n, that include basic looping functionality as well. While they both allow you to record phrases and add overdubs like most basic loopers—the Zoom G3n also allows for UNDO (see below)—their looping time is considerably shorter than most dedicated loopers. The RP360 allows for 40 seconds of looping time, while the Zoom allows for twice that. This is certainly plenty of time for a long riff, but it may not be enough time for a verse, pre-chorus, and chorus, for example. So while these multi-effect units may seem like a one-stop-shop if you only have basic looping needs—and they certainly are impressive with all they can do—you'll want to check the recording time and their list of features before assuming they'll do everything you need.

Digitech RP360XP

Add Overdubs

Overdubbing (or *layering*) is another indispensable function for a looper, and any unit on the market today will usually allow for infinite overdubbing. In other words, after laying down the first loop—a chord progression, for example—you can layer a bass line on top of it. Then, you could layer a riff on top of that, etc. With this function, you're able to create incredibly complex loops with only a very basic looper.

Stop/Start Playback

This simply means that, after you've set up your loop, you're able to stop it from playing back and then start it up again later. This is another crucial feature because it allows you more freedom with regards to the form of a song. In other words, if you have a loop that functions as the bed for the verse and chorus, but the bridge uses a different chord progression, you can stop the loop at that point and play "live" for the bridge. Once the verse or chorus returns, you can start the loop again.

Clear Loop

Another obvious feature, *CLEAR* allows you to completely erase the loop that's stored in the memory and start from scratch with a new loop. This should not be confused with *UNDO* (see the next page), which is not a global erasure of the looper's memory.

That's pretty much it as far as the bare necessities. In other words, in order for a unit to be referred to as looper, it's going to be able to record/play back a loop indefinitely, and it'll allow you to layer (usually limitless) overdubs on top of that loop. Now let's talk about a few more of the bells and whistles you're likely to see on most units.

Additional Features

Here, we'll look at the next level of complexity with regards to looping features. Many units will feature most of these, but always be sure to do your research before assuming something. Sometimes, you'll be surprised by what features a certain unit lacks or includes.

Undo

This somewhat understated feature is incredibly important and useful. It allows you to clear the previously recorded overdub without clearing the entire loop. Almost all dedicated loopers will have an *UNDO* function. In other words, let's say you lay down a strumming riff for the initial loop. Next, you overdub a bass line. Then, you add a melody on top, but you're not satisfied with it. You can remove that melody while leaving the original strumming riff and bass line intact.

This feature is an important safeguard that allows you to avoid a mistake being repeated over and over again throughout the whole song. Experienced looping artists will make use of this feature without the audience even knowing it. They may start to overdub a layer but make a mistake in the process, quickly undoing it before it's ever added to the loop. This requires some quick thinking and decision making. It's kind of like when you start playing a song and notice that one of your guitar strings is slightly out of tune. You have to quickly decide whether you can live with it or not. With the UNDO function, at least you won't have to start the whole loop over, but you will need to repeat that layer before moving on.

Redo

The *REDO* function is kind of the opposite of UNDO. It will add a previously "undone" layer back into the loop. This feature is a bit more exclusive than UNDO, and not all units with an UNDO feature will include REDO. While it may seem at first like something catering to a wishy-washy loop artist who can't decide whether or not to include the last layer, REDO can actually be a useful tool for adding or removing another layer of complexity to a loop.

Let's say you build a loop that includes a guitar riff, a bass line, and a melodic line. You could overdub a high ostinato part, for example on top of it, that you only want present during the chorus. Once the verse comes around, you can UNDO the ostinato part. At the chorus, you can REDO it, and so on.

The Boss RC-1 Loop Station allows for both UNDO and REDO functions.

Storable Loops

One feature that's very important to many performers is access to *storable loops*. In other words, the looper's memory can store more than one loop at a time. (Note that this doesn't mean it can play back more than one loop at a time; that's a feature we'll refer to as *multi-track capability*.) With this feature, you could have several loops stored in the pedal—one for each song in a set, perhaps—and switch between them as needed.

It's important to know the process used for selecting the different loops. Most importantly, some units—usually those with more than one footswitch—allow you to do this with your feet. Other units, such as the Electro-Harmonix Nano Looper 360, require you to rotate a knob to select the stored loop. While this isn't too much of a problem if you're only using one loop per song, it makes it very difficult to use two different stored loops for one song—using Loop 1 for an A section and Loop 2 for a B section, for example. If the ability to store/recall multiple loops is important to you, be sure to keep this in mind when choosing a looper.

The Nano Looper 360 from Electro-Harmonix allows you to store 11 loops in its internal memory.

One other thing to consider is whether or not the stored loops can be backed up to a computer, for example. Some units feature a USB port for connecting to a computer, or even a slot for an SDHC card, both of which allow you to offload unused loops to a backup device and access them later. The Digitech JamMan Solo XT allows for the storage of 200 loops in its internal memory, and it also has a card slot for additional storage.

External Footswitch Capability

This is a great option to have because it normally means you'll have foot-switchable access to features that otherwise require you to bend down and use your hands. Again, this is not just matter of laziness; it could mean the difference between being able to perform a certain song and not. One of the main features that's usually available with an external footswitch is the ability to cue up another stored loop (if your looper allows the storing of multiple loops). If you have one loop set for a verse and another for the chorus, then you won't have time to bend down and turn a knob or push a button on your pedal.

On the Digitech JamMan Solo XT, loop selection is normally done via two small up/down buttons that are not foot-accessible. However, you can use an external footswitch, which will allow you to cue the next loop, among other things.

The Digitech JamMan Solo XT allows for hands-off cueing of stored loops by way of an optional external footswitch.

Multiple Footswitches

Units with more than one footswitch built in normally allow for more flexibility when it comes to many types of operation. Often times, one or both of the switches can be set to access various parameters within the unit, including stopping playback, selecting stored loops, triggering onboard effects (see below), and more. Granted, these units will take up a bit more real estate on your pedal board, but it's usually no more than what one unit plus an external footswitch would occupy (and sometimes less!).

Boss RC-30 Loop Station

Metronome

Since playing in time is a vital part of creating a loop that grooves, a metronome can be a nice feature. Many loopers feature metronomes that can be turned on or off, or they can be set to only be heard while recording, etc. On the more full-featured loopers, there's often a headphone jack, which usually allows for the metronome to be routed there. This way, the audience won't hear it.

Some loopers operate more in a tempo/bpm fashion, allowing you to use features like tap tempo to change the speed of the metronome or a recorded loop without changing the pitch, allowing for quick and precise tempo adjustments. You'll most likely find that, with very little practice, you won't have trouble creating a seamless loop at all, even without a metronome, but it is a nice feature if you'd like to be more surgical about setting tempos, etc.

Headphone/Aux/USB/MIDI

Many loopers will feature extra input/output jacks for more flexibility. A headphone jack allows you to build loops anywhere without needing an amp, or it can be used to hear the metronome without the audience hearing it. An auxiliary input allows you to plug in your phone or mp3 player and add backing tracks to your setup. Many loopers also feature USB connectivity, which is mainly used for exporting and importing loops to and from your computer. MIDI jacks allow you to connect your looper to other MIDI-speaking devices, such as a laptop or tablet running a DAW or a keyboard workstation, etc. This means you can sync your loops to other pre-recorded tracks, expanding your options tenfold.

Effects

Many loopers will also feature built-in effects that can be applied to the loop(s). Some of the most common effects are:

- *Reverse*: This effect plays back the loop in reverse. Most units will still allow you to overdub another layer while in reverse mode, which usually results in that overdub sounding in reverse when you go back to normal (forward) playback. This means that you can mix forward- and reverse-sounding phrases together.

- *Half Speed*: This plays the loop at half-speed. On some loopers, this will also result in the pitch of the loop dropping by an octave. Again, you can usually still record a new overdub in this mode, often resulting in a chipmunk-style sound when returning to normal playback.

- *Double Speed*: This is essentially the opposite of Half Speed, causing the loop to play twice as fast (and sometimes causing the pitch to go up an octave).

- *Octave*: This effect transposes the loop up or down an octave without affecting tempo.

- *Fade*: This effect will cause the loop to fade out and stop at the end of the phrase.

- *Hold/Stutter*: This effect—which usually requires you to hold a switch down—causes one section of a loop to play over and over again, often causing a stuttering effect. Many times, the length of the "held" section can be adjusted via tap tempo or a knob.

- *Filter Sweep*: This effect creates envelope filter effects often by synchronizing with the tempo of the loop.

- *Lo-Fi*: This effect purposely degrades the signal quality of the loop for a lo-fi character.

- *Delay*: This adds a delay to the loop, which is often set to a multiple (quarter note, eighth note, 16th note, etc.) of the tempo.

- *Tempo Shift*: This effect allows you to increase or decrease the tempo of the loop (in gradations other than just half or double speed) without altering pitch.

Built-in Drums, Samples, etc.

For those who don't want to create their own percussive sounds by beating on their acoustic or tapping on their electric pickups, etc., some loopers contain built-in drum sounds that can be added to your loops. Especially if you're going for a full one-man band performance, this can be a nice feature that can add some depth to your sound. The Digitech Trio+ Band Creator Plus even generates drums and bass sounds in numerous styles based on what you play.

Digitech's Trio+ Band Creator Plus can add drum and bass sounds to your loop based on what you play.

Mic Input

Some loopers have a built-in XLR mic input, allowing you to plug a mic directly into the looper. The benefit to this is that it allows you to add vocals (or other acoustic instruments that you can mic) to your loops and have them be in perfect sync. TC Helicon even has the Ditto Mic Looper, which is designed specifically for microphones and only features an XLR input and output. Paired with a quick-adjust microphone stand, it may be all you need if you use nothing but acoustic instruments (acoustic guitar, mandolin, ukulele, percussion, etc.) and vocals.

TC Electronic Ditto Mic Looper

Other more guitar-based loopers, such as the Boss RC-30 Loop Station, also contain mic inputs but don't have much in the way of vocal processing—i.e., no built-in reverb, delay, etc. This means that if you want to add reverb to your vocals, for instance, you'd need to do so somewhere else in the signal chain. However, if you want to step up a bit in price, there are some truly powerhouse units out there, such as the Boss RC-300 Loop Station and the TC Helicon VoiceLive 3 Extreme. Both of these units feature multi-track looping with three separate loops, full MIDI control, a full selection of onboard guitar effects and amp simulation, and a host of vocal effects as well. The VoiceLive 3 Extreme even takes it a step further and adds a full smart vocal harmony generator, allowing you to generate three-part harmonies on the spot. If you're looking for a one-stop shop for all your guitar/vocal/looping performance needs, it's hard to beat.

TC Helicon VoiceLive 3 Extreme

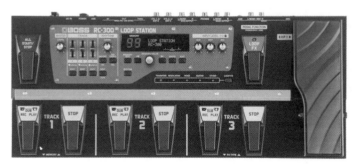

Boss RC-300 Loop Station

Multi-track Looping

I like to divide most loopers into two main groups: single-loop and multi-loop. *Multi-track looping* (or *multi-loop*) refers to a unit that's capable of playing back more than one loop at a time. Note that this is independent of a unit's ability to store multiple loops in its memory. For example, some units, such as the TC Electronic Ditto X4 Looper, allow for the playback of two different loops simultaneously—i.e., multi-track looping—but they don't allow for the storage of multiple loops in their internal memory for instant recall. (The Ditto X4 does allow you to export and import loops to and from a computer, but you can only have two loops in the unit at one time.)

Usually, if a looper has multi-track capability, you'll be able to stop and start playback of each loop independently of one another. In other words, if the unit has two loops, you could play back Loop 1, Loop 2, or both. Many units will allow you to set different lengths for each of the loops, which is a highly useful feature with regard to song form. For instance, maybe the verse loop is eight bars long, but the chorus loop needs to be 12 measures long. If this is important to you, make sure the looper you're considering has this feature.

The Ditto X4 Looper from TC Electronic allows for two independent loops to play back simultaneously or individually. Additionally, each loop can be a different length.

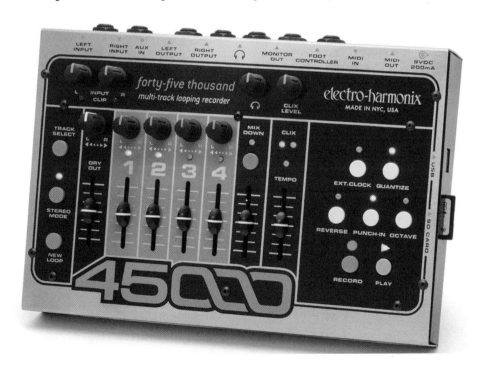

The 45000 Multi-track Looping Recorder from Electro-Harmonix allows individual playback of four loops. With an optional foot controller, the many of the features can be accessed hands-free.

Generally speaking, multi-track loopers are heavy on other features as well—such as effects, storable loops, etc.—but that's not always the case, so be sure to do your homework and make sure a unit has what you need before pulling the trigger.

Choosing the Right Looper

Now that we've examined most of the features available, let's quickly talk about how to choose the right looper for you. Everyone's needs are slightly different, just as every looper's feature set is slightly different, so it's important to look closely and think hard about what's a priority to you and what you can live without. So let's look at several common ways in which people tend to use loopers and discuss which features matter most.

Jamming or Practicing at Home

Some people don't care about performing so much and just like to have fun jamming at home. You may have heard that it's important to record yourself to hear how you sound, or maybe your guitar teacher wants you to practice playing over some backing tracks to work on your soloing. For this type of player, even the most basic of loopers will usually fit the bill perfectly. You can record yourself playing a chord progression or a riff and then solo over the top. Or, maybe you want to concentrate on singing and don't want to have to play the guitar at the same time. Loop a rhythm part and practice singing to your heart's content.

Any unit with basic looping functionality will work great for this type of thing. The only feature you may want to consider is the looping time. If you're wanting to record a particularly long chord progression, for example, you may need to get a dedicated looper, as opposed to using the loop function that comes on some multi-effects pedals.

Recommendations

- TC Electronic Ditto Looper
- Boss RC-1
- Digitech JamMan Express XT
- Electro-Harmonix Nano Looper 360

Songwriting and Storing Loops

Looper pedals can also be great songwriting tools, as many players use loops to get inspired when writing new songs. In this scenario, one of the most important features is the ability to store multiple loops and/or be able to transfer your loops to a computer for backup. The latter is the more important feature, since it's essentially limitless. Generally speaking, loopers that allow for the storage of many loops in their internal memories will also allow you for USB connectivity to back them up to a computer. However, there are some loopers that can't store multiple loops in their memory but can still transfer loops to a computer via USB.

Some other important features for this type of use would be UNDO and REDO, which will likely be included if the looper can store or transfer loops. Though not crucial, some loop effects would be a nice touch as well, as sometimes the right sound can inspire an entire song. (Of course, many users of a looper will have other effects pedals on their board as well.) If you're writing vocal songs—as opposed to just guitar riffs, etc.—a mic input would be very helpful as well, since you'd be able to use the looper as a scratchpad, quickly catching a complete idea all at once.

Recommendations

- Digitech JamMan Solo XT (guitar ideas only)
- TC Electronic Ditto Looper X2 (guitar ideas only)
- TC Electronic Ditto Mic Looper (vocals and acoustic instruments only)
- Boss RC-3 (guitar ideas only)
- Electro-Harmonix 22500 (guitar and vocals)
- Boss RC-30 (guitar and vocals)

Studio Recording and Guitar-based Performance

Some folks like to record in the studio with loopers, creating ambient, sound-on-sound textures or intricate, rhythmic compositions. While this may seem a bit unnecessary, as you can essentially create almost anything with a DAW that you could with a looper, the process is different when working with a looper. And for some people, the process is everything. For studio use, some important factors may be multi-track looping (though not always), effects, and multiple footswitches or external footswitch capability. In other words, you'd like access to a lot of sounds and textures in a timely fashion.

The same could be said of the limited performance scenario. By "guitar-based performance," I'm talking mostly about a loop artist who uses mostly instrumental loops (often guitar, but sometimes bass or keys, etc.) but doesn't use looping with regard to vocals. (They may sing over the top of the loop, but they don't loop the vocals.) One additional feature that's very useful in performance is the ability to store and recall multiple loops.

Recommendations

- TC Electronic Ditto X4 Looper
- Digitech JML2 JamMan
- Digitech Trio+ Band Creator Plus
- Boss RC-30
- Line 6 JM4
- Electro-Harmonix Grand Canyon
- Electro-Harmonix 45000 Multi-Track Looping Recorder

Full One-Man Band Performance: Vocals, Guitars, and More

If you're wanting to create a full, "one-man band" sound with instruments and vocals, then you should err on the side of the more features, the better. Multi-track looping, effects, multiple/external footswitches, and mic input are the norm with this kind of setup, and, as expected, you're going to have a spend a bit more money to get a unit with this many features.

It's also important to remember that this type of use often requires a good bit of preparation. You'll really need to learn the ins and outs of the unit in order to get the most out of it and its features. So expect a bit of a learning curve with these higher-end units. As they say, with great power comes great responsibility!

Recommendations

- TC Helicon VoiceLive3 Extreme
- Boss RC-300 Loop Station
- Headrush Looperboard

So we've talked about the various features available and how to choose the best looper for your needs. The next step is—if you haven't done so already—to go out and get yourself a looper! Meet me back at Chapter 2 after you do, and we'll start getting set up and ready to roll.

Chapter 2: Looping Rig Setups

OK, so you have your new looper, and you're ready to go. But how exactly do you set it up? Where in the signal chain do you place it? What goes into it and what goes out of it? Those are all great questions, and in this chapter, we're going to answer them. In fact, we'll see that—depending on the type of looper you have and what exactly you want to do with it—there are many possible answers to these questions.

So we're going to take a look at several common setups that involve using a looper and detail which plug goes where. We'll cover several different types of loopers—from the most basic to the most sophisticated—and explore some of the different options available with each. By the end of the chapter, you should be quite clear on how to set up your rig.

Basic Guitar Looper and Amp

*To access this video and others like it, head over to **www.halleonard.com/mylibrary** and input the code found on page 1!*

This is perhaps the most basic setup of all. You plug your guitar into the looper's input and then plug the looper's output into your amp's input. It doesn't get much more basic than this.

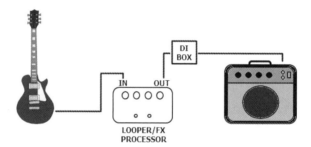

Note that, with this setup, when you change the tone of your amp, you will change the tone of your recorded loop as well because the change of tone is happening after the looper. So for example, if you record a loop with your amp set to the clean channel and then change to the distorted channel, the sound of your loop will change from clean to distorted as well.

Post-Effects Guitar Looper and Amp (Default Setup for Effects)

In this setup, you'll run from your guitar through your effects chain, then through the looper, and finally, to the amp. Placing the looper at the end of your signal chain—i.e., right before the amp—is the most common when using effects. This is because any effect you use before the looper—delay, phaser, distortion, tremolo, reverb, etc.—will get recorded by the looper and will then be "printed" in the loop.

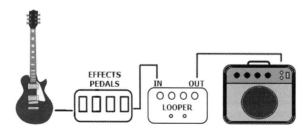

For example, you could record the initial loop with a phaser. Then, you could turn the phaser off and turn on a tremolo effect to record the overdub. The initial loop will still feature the phaser effect, but the overdub will feature the tremolo effect.

Keep in mind that, if your looper has a mic input too, you'll need to check on whether or not the mic and guitar signals are summed for the output. If they are, then any effect you apply to the guitar before the looper will most likely be applied to the mic as well.

Pre-Effects Guitar Looper and Amp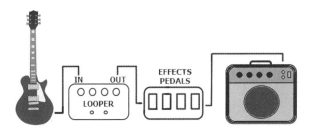

This is the same as the previous setup, except that the looper is located before your effects pedals.

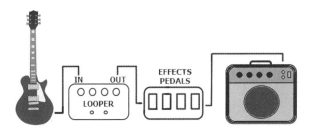

With this setup, any effect changes you make will affect everything in the recorded loop. For example, if you recorded the initial loop with a phaser effect and then wanted to add an overdub with a tremolo effect, you won't be able to do it. As soon as you change from the phaser to the tremolo, the loop is going to change to the tremolo effect. This is because you recorded a dry (unaffected) guitar signal in the looper—because the looper was placed immediately after your guitar—and now you're processing that dry signal by adding/removing effects to/from it. So even though you recorded that first loop while you had a phaser sound, the looper didn't record the phaser effect; it just recorded your dry guitar signal, which happened to be processed with a phaser somewhere later in the signal chain.

This setup does have its uses, however. It's great for auditioning sounds, for example. You can record a riff and loop it while you make effects adjustments until you find the sound you're looking for. This allows you to get really hands-on with the effects and not have to worry about playing the same riff hundreds of times.

This is also a nice setup if you really want to get creative with your knob tweaking and just create some music with effects alone. For example, you could setup one or two loops—switching from one to the next or playing them both together—and have them playback while you manipulate, mangle, and twist them with your choice of effects.

Mic Looper and PA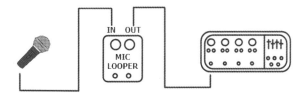

This is a basic setup for using a mic looper with a PA system without any effects. In other words, any effects that are added would be done by onboard or external mixer effects from the PA system. You simply run from the mic to the looper's input and then from the looper's output to the mic input on a PA channel.

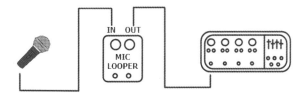

Post-Effects Mic Looper and PA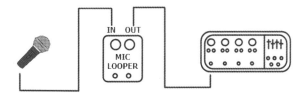

In this setup, we've added an effects processor between the mic and the mic looper. In this setup, any effects you use to record with will be "printed" on the loop and will remain, even if you change effects later. There are many dedicated vocal effects processors for this type of setup. These processors will typically have XLR inputs and outputs so that you won't need to use any special type of adapter. This is the easiest, no-hassle way to add effects to your mic looper that you can easily control on stage.

The Mic Mechanic by TC Helicon is one such device. With several choices for echo/delay and reverb, as well as adjustable pitch correction (from none to 100% robot style), it's an awesome little unit that gives you a lot of flexibility when you want control over your vocal effects. It also features a one-button "Tone" control that simultaneously adds compression, EQ, de-essing, and gating for a more polished, professional sound.

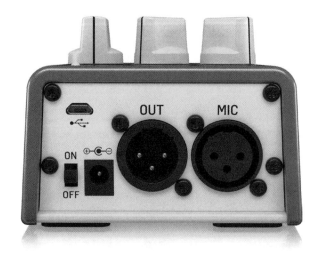

TC Helicon Mic Mechanic

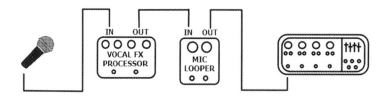

But what about your favorite guitar effect pedals? Can you use them with your mic looper as well? The short answer is yes, but it requires a few additions in the signal chain. You'll need to use a few impedance transformer adapters to convert the signal from mic level to guitar level and back again. (If you have two DI boxes, this will accomplish the same thing.) You'll need two adapters for this:

- XLR female to 1/4" male

- 1/4" female to XLR male

Hosa MIT-435 XLR Female LO-Z to 1/4"
TS Male HI-Z Microphone
Input Impedance Transformer

Hosa MIT-129 XLR Male LO-Z to 1/4"
TS Female HI-Z Microphone
Input Impedance Transformer

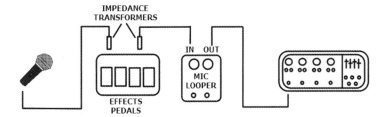

Pre-Effects Mic Looper and PA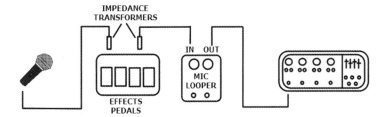

With this setup, we're simply placing the mic looper before the effects instead of after. As with the pre-effects guitar looper setup, this will mean that no effects will be "printed" in the loop. The uses again include:

- Auditioning of effects or tones without having to sing/play the same thing over and over

- Hands-on experimenting with sound shaping and mangling

It's actually pretty fun to take a looped vocal phrase and subject it to a string of guitar pedals to see what you can do with it!

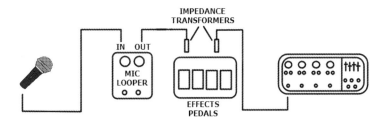

Guitar/Mic Looper and PA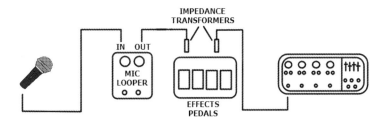

In this setup, you'll use a looper that contains effects and amp simulation for your guitar sound—no amp required. Instead, you'd use a stage monitor to hear yourself. If the unit has a mic input, you can loop vocals and mic'd instruments, too. Usually, all the effects will come from the unit itself, but you can still run other pedals in front or behind if you'd like. Just remember that any effects before the looper will be printed on the loops; any effects after the looper will not be printed on the loops.

If your unit doesn't have an XLR output, you'll usually need to use a DI box when running from the looper into the PA. Of course, if it's a venue with its own sound equipment, the sound man will normally have this. It never hurts to be prepared, though. (You can use an impedance transformer adapter as well.) If you have an XLR out, a DI box won't be required.

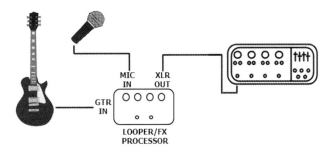

Guitar/Mic Looper and PA with Amp ▶

Finally, this setup is for use with looper/multi-effects units that have separate mic and guitar outputs. You can run from the mic output to the PA and from the guitar output to your amp. This offers more flexibility with regards to using separate effects for guitar and mic. With this setup, remember to turn off the amp simulator effect in your looper/multi-effect unit, since you'll be using an actual guitar amp. Units like this will almost always have an XLR out for the mic channel and a 1/4" out for the guitar channel.

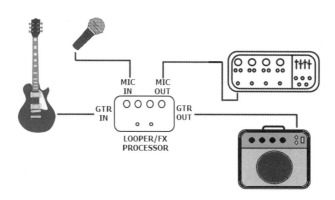

Of course, all of these setups are basic starting points. There are many other possibilities, but most of them will basically act as variations on one of these themes. Feel free to experiment as necessary to get the sounds and flexibility you need.

Chapter 3: Basic Looping Techniques

You're all set up and ready to go, so let's get to it! In this chapter, we're going to be looking at some basic looping techniques and what we can do with them. To start, we'll be dealing exclusively with single-loop techniques here. In other words, we're using a looper than can only play back one loop at a time. (We'll deal with multiple loops later in the book.)

Know Your Looper

As we discussed in Chapter 1, there are a lot of loopers out there, and they don't all work the same. I'm going to be demonstrating the looping techniques in this book and the accompanying video with loopers from TC Electronic (Ditto X4 Looper) and TC Helicon (Ditto Mic Looper and VoiceLive 3 Extreme), and I'll show you how to accomplish these techniques on those units. But your looper may work slightly differently. Therefore, it's important that you crack open the manual for your looper if necessary so you know how to do these things on your unit.

Most loopers on the market today—especially the more basic ones—are designed to be as intuitive as possible. But on units with only one footswitch, I guarantee you that it serves more than one function. You'll most likely need to use various combinations of single-push, double-push, push-and-hold, etc. in order to achieve these techniques. The manual for your specific looper should make all of this clear.

The First Loop ▶

The first step is to set up the original loop. From there, we can do several things, including:

- Play or sing "live" over the top.

- Clear the loop from memory to create a new one.

- Overdub more layers.

- Undo and/or redo the top layer.

- Stop the loop to play something different live, and then start it again at a later point.

We're going to look at all of these options, but first thing's first: We need a loop. (Note: If you haven't checked out the "Notational Conventions" on page 4 yet, be sure to do that now.) So let's start with something simple. We have our looper in the default setup for this—i.e., at the end of our pedal chain—which means that the original loop we create will continue to sound the same even if we change effects for overdubs. I'll be using the TC Electronic Ditto X4 for this in the video. (Note that, although the Ditto X4 is actually a two-track looper, I'll only be using the first loop and will therefore be treating it as a single-loop unit for this chapter.)

Let's start with this eighth-note riff in A here.

Example 3-1

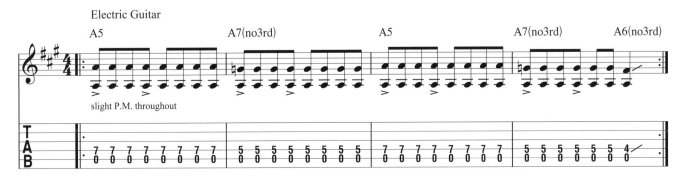

Gear Spotlight: TC Electronic Ditto X4 Looper

The Ditto X4 is a two-loop pedal that allows for severely creative looping. The loops can be used in serial mode (one plays after the other) or sync mode (both play simultaneously), with either one able to be turned on or off independently in both modes. You get five minutes of recording time per loop, and there are also seven built-in effects—including Reverse, Half/Double Speed, Tape Stop, Fade, and more—that can be applied to the loops, allowing for a host of sonic possibilities. The unit features four footswitches: LOOP 1, LOOP 2, STOP, and FX. Taken together, they afford an enormous amount of control without ever having to bend down and get your hands dirty. The Ditto X4 also allows you to transfer your loops to and from your computer, and you can also load two backing tracks (one per loop), over which you can simply play or build loops. MIDI IN and THRU jacks also allow for perfect loop synchronization when incorporating another device with MIDI clock, such as a synth or DAW.

Looping Tip!

When setting up a loop, it's best to start with something that's rhythmically active if possible. This will make it easier to create solid starting and ending points. So if you're wanting to create a loop with an eighth-note riff, some whole-note chord strums, and a melody, it's best to start with the eighth-note riff as opposed to the whole-note strums, for example.

For most loop pedals, this will involve pressing the footswitch once to start recording. On some loopers, recording will start right away once you push the footswitch. On others, recording will start once the looper "hears" you start playing. On the Ditto X4, recording starts right with the footswitch push, so you need to time it properly. This will take just a bit of practice, but it will soon become second nature.

Once you have the timing down, start recording the loop and then stop recording precisely at the end of it. On the Ditto X4, you start recording by pressing the LOOP 1 footswitch (the light will turn red) and stop recording by pressing the same switch again. The light will turn from red to green once you stop recording, and the loop will already be in playback mode. (Notice the "Start Loop 1" and "End Loop 1" indications in the music.)

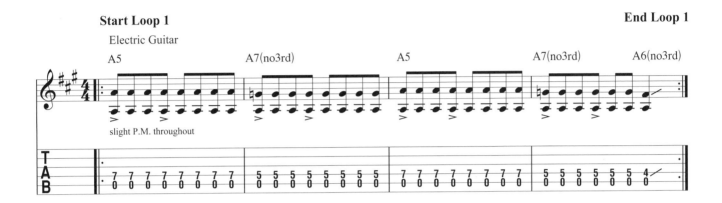

Looping Tip!

To help develop the timing for starting a loop, it may help to play the riff first without recording instead of just trying to start cold. In other words, start playing the riff and get your foot ready to push the button. Then, when you reach the end of the riff, push the button to start recording when you begin to repeat the riff. Once you reach the spot where the riff would start again, press the button to stop recording. Essentially, the start and stop button pushes will essentially take place at the same spot within the riff.

As mentioned earlier, it may take a bit of practice to get a smooth loop. It boils down to two things:

- Playing in time.
- Timing the in (start recording) and out (stop recording) points properly.

I haven't mentioned it yet, but having good time (tempo) is extremely important when playing with a looper. Unlike playing live, any timing error that's incorporated into the loop will play over and over again, hanging around like the smell from a dead animal under the house. The UNDO function can help with that, but if you don't notice something right away and miss your chance to undo a layer before adding another one, it'll be too late.

Therefore, it goes without saying that you want a solid time feel. The absolute best way to get that is to practice with a metronome or drum machine—i.e., something that will keep a steady, unwavering beat. If you've never played with a metronome before, it can sometimes be quite alarming the first time you do. Recording yourself while playing with a metronome will give you even more objectivity because you'll solely be listening, as opposed to trying to listen while you're still playing.

Once you've developed a good sense of time, then it all comes down to nailing the in and out points on the footswitch. This just takes a bit of practice; before you know it, you won't have to think about it at all.

Playing Over the Top ▶

So now we have a simple, four-bar loop that will play until we tell it to stop. If we just want to practice soloing, then we're good to go. You let the loop play and solo away! Here's an example of that.

w/ Loop 1

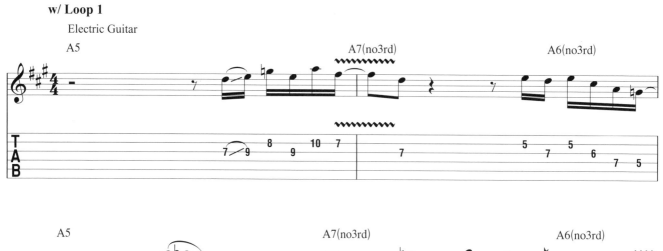

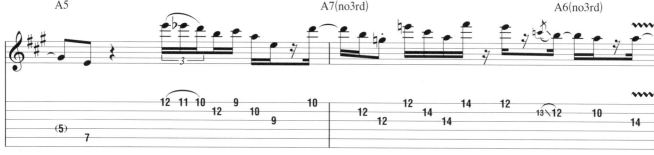

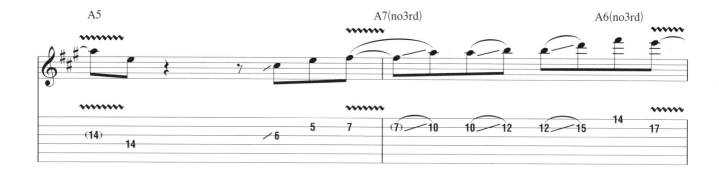

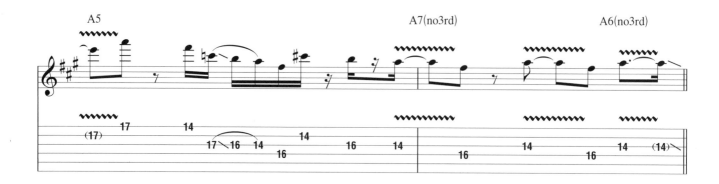

Clearing the Loop ▶

So you have a great little phrase-trainer in your loop pedal. Maybe you want to practice your ii–V–I licks now? You just clear the loop and create a new one. With the Ditto X4, this is done by first stopping playback (press the STOP switch or double press the LOOP 1 switch) and then pushing and holding the LOOP 1 footswitch. (It will likely be something similar if you have a different looper.) The green light will go out on the Ditto X4, indicating that there is no loop in the memory.

Now you're ready to create a new loop. How about practicing some ii–V–I licks?

Example 3-2

If you'd like to create more elaborate practice tracks, you can do so by adding more layers to the loop. And that's where we're headed next.

Overdubbing Layers ▶

Of course, your looper is much more than a jam track. Much of the fun of a looper can be had by experimenting with endless overdubs in real time. To demonstrate overdubbing, I'll set up this new loop here in E minor.

Example 3-3

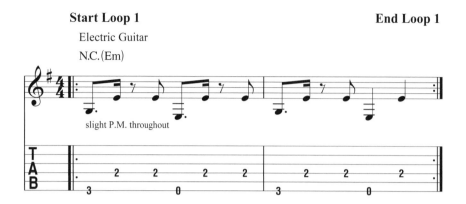

So we have this cool, bassline riff. In order to overdub another layer on the Ditto X4, we start playing the loop (if it's not already) and then just press the LOOP 1 switch again. The light turns from green to red, indicating that we're in recording mode again, and we're ready to overdub. (This is also sometimes referred to as "punching in.") Wait until the beginning of the loop comes around and then add this melody on top.

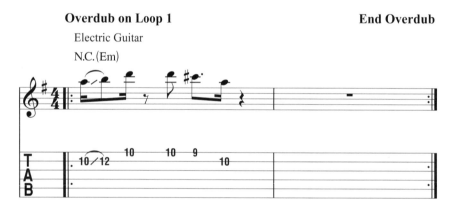

After playing the melody, you stop recording and enter playback mode again. (This is also referred to as "punching out.") On the Ditto X4, we just press the LOOP 1 switch again—the light will turn green again to indicate playback mode. You've now successfully added your first overdub.

Looping Tip!

Especially in loopers with only one footswitch, understand that the switch will often pull triple duty or more regarding functionality. It's up to you to read the manual and find out how it works. There are several types of "pushes" you may need to perform on a unit with a single footswitch, including:

- Single push
- Double push
- Single push and hold
- Double push and hold

Not all loopers will use all of these, but many will. Depending on the mode your looper is in, these types of actions will perform different functions. Again, performing with a looper takes a good amount of preparation. Know your looper!

Undo and Redo

So let's say you weren't pleased with the performance of the first overdub. That's no problem; there's no need to start all over from scratch. Most loopers have an UNDO function that will remove the most recently recorded overdub but leave everything else in the loop intact. You'll need to consult the manual on your looper to find out exactly how to do this. On the Ditto X4, this is accomplished by pushing and holding the LOOP 1 switch for 1.5 seconds or longer during playback. (If you push and hold the LOOP 1 switch while the loop is stopped, then you'll clear the loop. Again, this is why it's important to know your looper!)

So you've undone the first overdub, leaving the original bass riff intact. Now you can record the overdub again (and again and again if necessary) until you get it right. If you decide that—"You know what? Maybe I was a bit hasty in deleting that overdub. Maybe it wasn't as bad as I thought!"—then most loopers allow you to REDO it. On the Ditto X4, this is done by the same method as UNDO; simply push and hold the LOOP 1 switch while in playback mode. So you can add the last layer back in and see if it really needed to be deleted or not.

So now let's double our melody an octave higher by overdubbing again.

That sounds nice, but we have a big hole in the second half of the riff that sounds a bit empty. So let's add another melody there with another overdub.

And how about we harmonize that last melody with yet another overdub?

Now let's sit back and check out what we've built. Here are all five parts we recorded!

Stopping the Loop to Play "Live" ▶

Sometimes you'll need to stop the loop within a song for various reasons. This could be because you need to play a new chord progression for another song section, or maybe you just want to create some dynamics by having the bottom drop out for a spell. All loopers will allow you to stop the loop, obviously, but there's one important thing to consider: When exactly do you want the loop to stop?

Do you want to stop it immediately, or you do you want to stop it once it reaches the end of the looped phrase? There are usually two different procedures for this, depending on your looper. Some loopers will only be able to do one of these options. Consult your manual to find out what your looper will do.

Stopping the Loop at the End of the Phrase

First, let's consider the more common approach: stopping the loop at the end of the phrase. On the Ditto X4—when you're in Serial mode (we'll talk more about this later)—there are two ways to stop the loop at the end of the phrase. You can either double-press the LOOP 1 switch, or you can simply press the STOP switch. Doing either one of these actions will allow the looper to finish its current phrase and stop at the end. The benefit to this method is that you don't have to time the stop, which allows you to concentrate on what you'll be playing next. (If your looper does not allow for this feature, then you'll simply need to time the button push when stopping the loop. It's not as convenient, but it's certainly doable.)

Let's demonstrate this by setting up the following three-layer loop.

Example 3-4

So let's say we want to stop this loop at the end of the phrase so we can play a new figure. We would use this first method so we can drop in with a live riff once the loop stops. Then, we would start the loop again with a timed button push. (Turn to the next page to see this in action.)

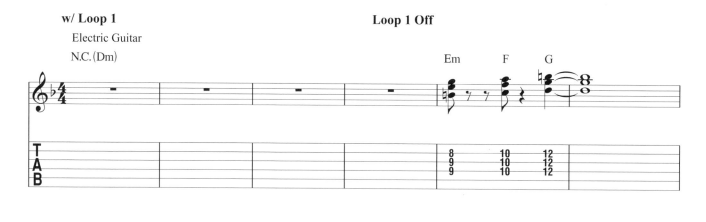

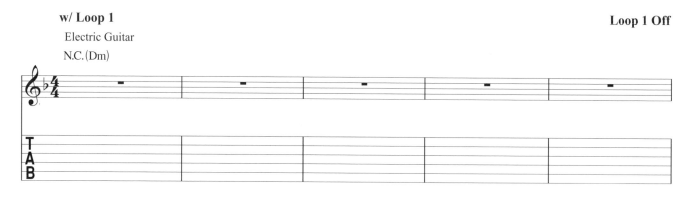

Stopping the Loop Immediately

Sometimes, you need to stop the loop immediately—i.e., before it reaches the end of the phrase. On the Ditto X4, this is done by double pressing the STOP switch. This is nice for when you want the bottom to drop out dramatically for a fill, for example.

Let's stop the loop after one measure and add a two-measure fill before starting the loop again.

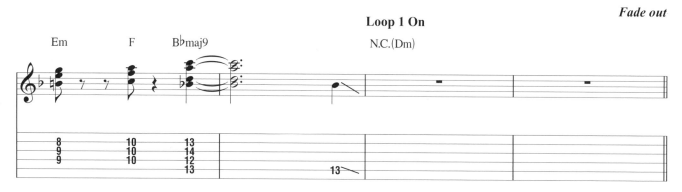

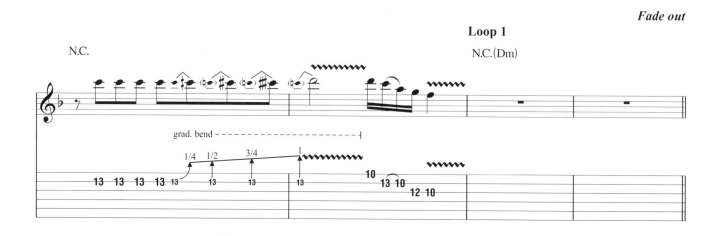

Looping Practice ▶

So that pretty much sums up the basic functions found on most loopers out there. Let's build one more loop from the ground up for good measure. We'll use this as an opportunity to practice some of the techniques we've learned in this chapter. Here's what we'll do:

- Build a four-layer loop.
- Stop the loop at a specific point (indicated in the music) and play a fill.
- Start the loop again after the fill.
- Undo the fourth layer of the loop.
- Play a brief solo over the remaining loop.

Here we go!

Example 3-5

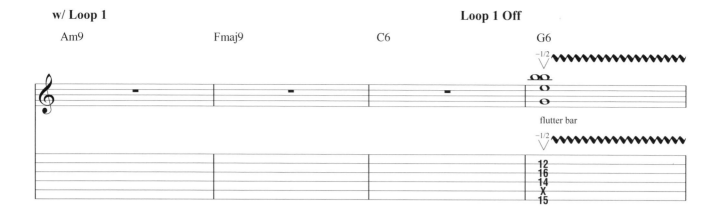

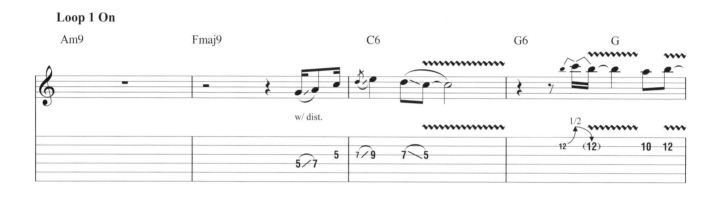

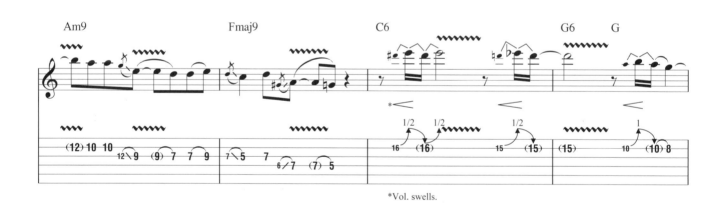

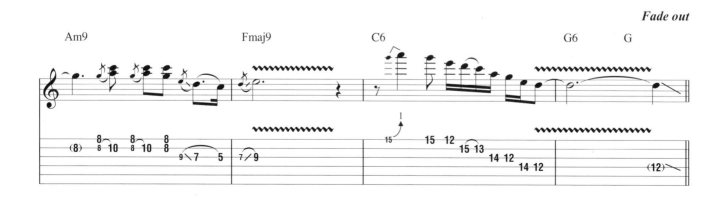

A Few More Thoughts on Undo and Redo

Since these are such powerful and often-overlooked functions of a looper, let's spend just a bit more time working with them before we move on. There are a few more aspects of each that merit a closer look.

Overdubbing More than One Layer at a Time

This is a feature that may not be present on every looper, so consult your manual to see how your specific unit operates. Here's the scenario I'm talking about. Let's say you've recorded your basic loop, like the example below.

Example 3-6

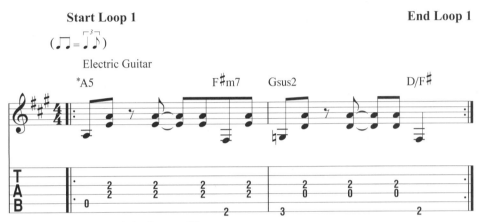

*Chord symbols reflect overall harmony.

And now you're ready to lay down some overdubs. On the Ditto X4, if the loop is playing back (the light is green), you simply press the LOOP 1 switch again to arm it for recording an overdub (the light will turn to red). Here's the thing, though: If you don't stop recording by the end of the loop cycle, the Ditto X4 will keep adding overdubs on top until you do stop. In other words, if you start overdubbing and then play through two full loop cycles before punching out, it will add everything you played to the loop.

For example, let's say you record something like the example below.

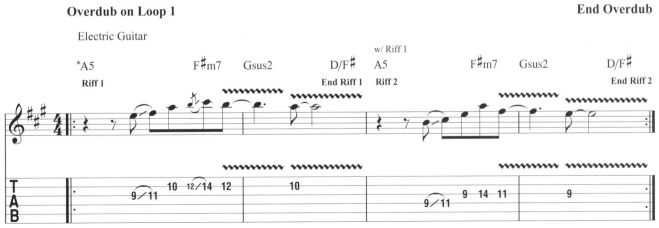

*Chord symbols reflect overall harmony.

Notice that, although the loop is only two measures long, we overdubbed for four measures before punching out. On the Ditto X4, this will result in the following layers in the loop.

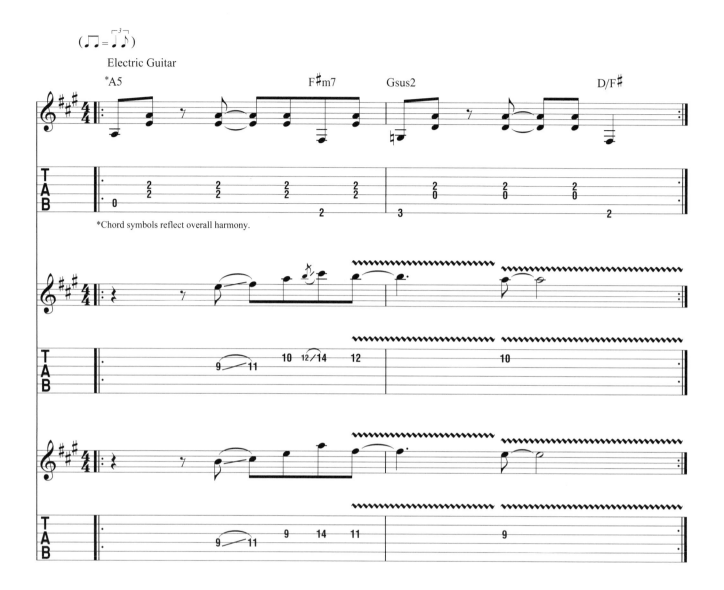

*Chord symbols reflect overall harmony.

OK, so that's cool, right? It allows you to overdub a bunch of layers quickly without worrying about tap dancing for a while. But there's a catch to this method. If you now use the UNDO function, you'll undo those entire four measures of overdub. In other words, you'd be left with the original loop only.

So the UNDO function doesn't just undo the last loop cycle of overdub; it undoes everything that was recorded last before you punch out. Again, this is the way the Ditto X4 functions. Some loopers may not function this way, so be sure to check the manual before you hit the stage!

Using Undo and Redo Creatively ▶

As I mentioned earlier in the book, the UNDO and REDO functions aren't only useful for removing a mistake or adding a layer back that wasn't too bad after all. You can also use them in a creative manner in which they almost serve like a separate loop.

Here's what I mean. Let's say you've built this three-layer loop, which serves as the verse in the song on the next page.

Example 3-7

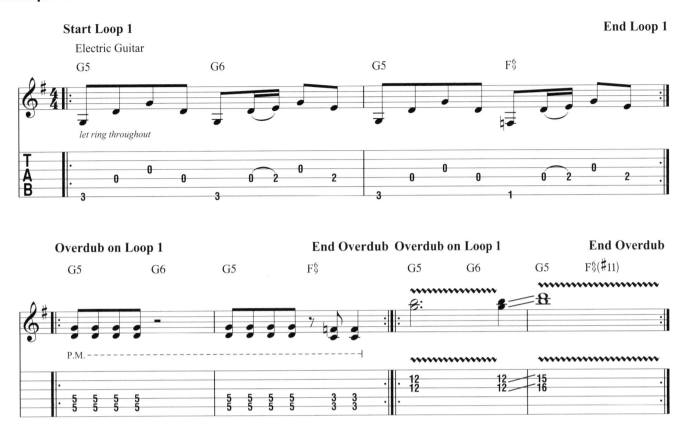

And now let's say you want to add some excitement to the chorus by adding an octave part. You can overdub another layer, like in this next example.

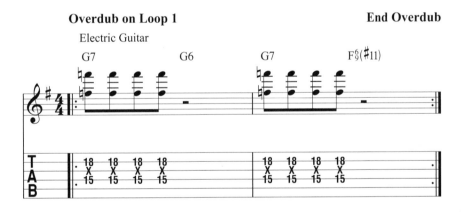

After the chorus is done, you can use the UNDO function to remove the chorus part, leaving the original verse loop as it was. Then, when the chorus comes back around, you can use REDO to bring back that octave part. You can even embolden it more if you'd like by playing a harmony octave with it! Here's an example.

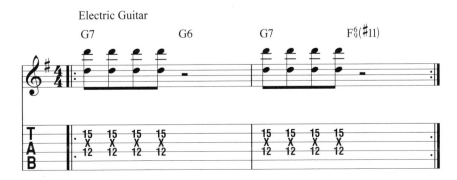

And of course, if your looper acts as the Ditto X4 with regard to the previous technique of overdubbing more than one layer at a time without stopping, this can be even more of a dramatic effect. You could have, for example, three different guitar parts join in for the chorus and then disappear again for the verse, etc. Use your imagination!

Undone Before You Know It ▶️

Once you get the hang of the UNDO function, you can become pretty sly about covering up your mistakes. For example, it's possible to start overdubbing, make a mistake, punch out, UNDO that mistake, and be ready to start overdubbing again before the loop cycle ends.

Here's an example. First, we'll lay down a simple, A minor chord riff.

Example 3-8

And now we'll try overdubbing this line. But we'll purposely make a mistake while doing it. The idea is this: When you make a mistake, keep playing as if nothing happened, but press UNDO immediately after the mistake (while you're playing). Then, be ready to punch in before the loop cycle begins again. To the audience, it will most likely just look and sound as though you played the same thing twice.

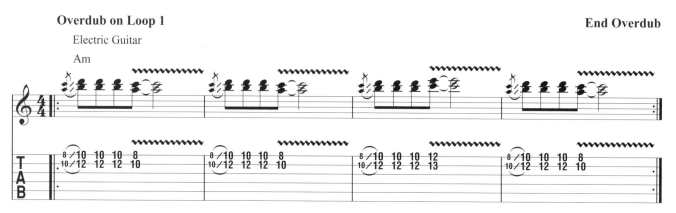

On the Ditto X4, the sequence of actions would be as follows:

- Press LOOP 1 switch to punch in (start overdubbing).

- Realize you've made a mistake (but keep playing!).

- Press LOOP 1 switch again to punch out (stop overdubbing).

- Press and hold LOOP 1 switch for UNDO function.

- Press LOOP 1 switch at end of loop cycle to punch in again.

Repeat this move until you're able to get it seamless. The sequence of button pushing won't take long to learn at all. What will likely take a bit of practice is to do it all while you keep playing. A veteran loop artist will do this kind of thing without thinking about it, but in the beginning, it'll take a bit of getting used to. It's often instinctive to stop playing if we make a mistake while recording something, but in the case of live performance, of course, that's not always desirable.

Of course, if you make a mistake near the very end of the loop cycle, you may not have time to do this. But there will be plenty of times that you will. Getting into the habit will make your performances more polished and seamless.

Chapter 4: Incorporating a Mic Looper ▶

Using a mic looper will allow you to add a host of other sounds to your loops, including vocals, percussion, and a whole slew of other acoustic instruments (guitar, mandolin, ukulele, banjo, etc.). While some more affordable loopers—such as the Boss RC-30 or Electro-Harmonix 22500—come with mic inputs, enabling you to loop both guitar and vocals at the same time, there are other options out there as well for those of you wanting to add some organic sounds to your loops.

I'll be demonstrating the techniques in this chapter with a Ditto Mic Looper from TC Helicon. With regard to the looping, it works almost the same the same as the Ditto X4:

- Press LOOP to start recording, press LOOP again to stop recording (and start playback).

- While it's in playback mode, press LOOP to start overdubbing and LOOP again to stop overdubbing.

- To stop the loop, press STOP.

- To UNDO (or REDO) the previous layer, press and hold the LOOP switch.

- To clear the loop, press and hold STOP.

Gear Spotlight: TC Helicon Ditto Mic Looper

The Ditto Mic Looper is a simple-yet-powerful, single-loop unit for use with a microphone. In other words, if you can stick a mic in front of it, you can loop it! Although it sports a small footprint, it features two footswitches, which makes operation easy and intuitive. The LOOP switch handles the playback, recording, and UNDO/REDO duties, while the STOP switch handles the stop and loop-clearing functions. Easy! As with the Ditto X4, you get five minutes of loop time, and you can transfer your loops to and from the computer via USB. A color-coded LED makes it clear what's happening at any time. The pedal is built like a tank and features XLR inputs and outputs. Simply plug a mic in and then run a mic cable to your PA (or audio interface if you're recording), and you're ready to go!

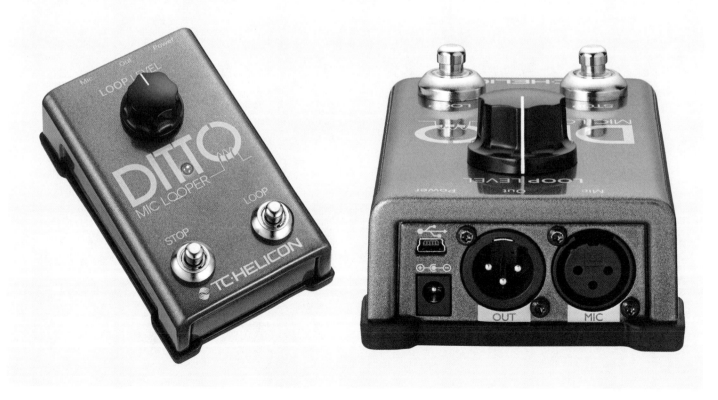

Creating an Acoustic Loop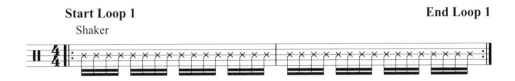

Now let's have some fun with some acoustic instruments and vocals. Much of the looping techniques here will be similar to the previous chapter, but using a mic presents a few new elements.

Starting with Percussion

Having a mic at the ready means we can record some auxiliary percussion sounds. Let's set up a percussion loop here, using a shaker first. Then, we'll add bongos and simulate a bass drum and snare with an acoustic guitar.

First up is a shaker. On the Ditto Mic Looper, we push the LOOP switch when we're ready to record and push it again when we're done.

Example 4-1

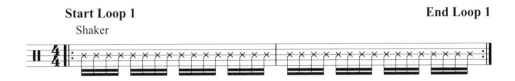

Think Ahead!

It's important to exercise a little forethought when setting up a percussion loop as the first thing. This is because, although the percussion part may only be a one-measure pattern, the chord progression or riff that's going over the top may be two measures long. Therefore, you need to make the percussion loop as long as the riff or chord progression. Otherwise, if you just loop a one-measure part for the percussion, you'll be stuck with that phrase length when you overdub anything else.

Of course, this only applies to single-loop devices. If you have a multi-track looper, then you'll likely be able to set up another loop that's a multiple of the first loop. The other option is to set up the riff or chord progression first and then add the percussion last. This is perhaps the best option if you don't have something already planned and are just improvising.

Notice that, although the shaker plays the same thing in each measure, we made the loop two measures long so that we can overdub a two-measure riff or chord progression later. How about some bongos next? Push the LOOP switch on the Ditto Mic Looper to start playback, push it again to start recording, and overdub away!

Next, let's add the simulated bass and snare. You can do this in a number of ways with an acoustic. I like to use my palm on the front of the guitar for the bass drum sound and then slap the side for the snare sound. If the Ditto Mic Looper is in playback mode, we push the LOOP switch to start overdubbing and push it again when you're done.

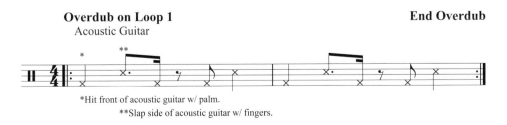

*Hit front of acoustic guitar w/ palm.
**Slap side of acoustic guitar w/ fingers.

Of course, if you have a cajón lying around—or even a bass and a real snare—you can use those instead. I demonstrated here with an acoustic because:

- If you're a guitar player, you'll already have it with you.

- You won't have to move the mic around after recording the shaker.

But that's the beauty of the mic looper; you can throw a mic on just about anything! (This includes an electric guitar amp, of course; we'll talk about that later.)

Adding Acoustic Guitar

Now we'll add an acoustic guitar riff over the percussion loop. Since we made the percussion loop two measures long, we can create a two-measure riff. Let's overdub that by pushing the LOOP switch while the loop is playing. Push it again to punch out.

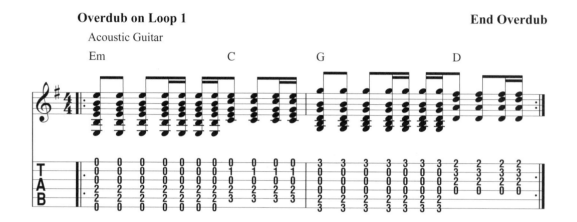

Adding Backing Vocals

Next up, let's add a couple of harmonized backing vocals using the same process. We'll likely need to adjust the mic stand a bit to do this. If you plan on doing this type of thing often, you'll probably want to invest in a quick-release mic stand that adjusts quickly via a trigger motion. With this type of stand, you simply squeeze a trigger, and you're able to raise and lower the stand with one hand.

The Hercules EZ-Grip stand allows for quick, one-handed height adjustment.

It's important to remember that UNDO will work differently depending on how you record these backing vocals. If you want to be able to undo both backing vocals at once, then you'll want to press LOOP, overdub the first part, and continue to overdub the second part on the next cycle. Then, you punch out. By doing that, you can use UNDO to remove the backing vocals as one unit when you don't want them and then bring them back in with REDO when you do want them.

Here's the first part:

And now the second:

And there you have it—a nice five-layer loop containing the following:

- Shaker

- Bass/snare simulation

- Bongos

- Acoustic guitar

- Two backing vocals

Adding a Mic Mixer for More Flexibility ▶

The main limitation to using a mic looper is that the mic needs to be where the sound source is. As mentioned earlier, a quick-release stand is certainly helpful in this regard, but there's another alternative that allows for even more flexibility: using an external *mixer* or *mic mixer*.

This allows you to have several mics already set up at different heights, etc. so that you can move from instrument to instrument without having to make any stand adjustments. It could simply be as few as two mics: one for vocals and one for acoustic guitar, for example. Or, it could entail four mics or more. However many mics you use, you'll submix them and then run one output from the mixer into the mic looper.

To demonstrate this idea, let's create another loop using the Ditto Mic Looper, but this time we'll submix three mics:

- Mic 1 will be used for acoustic guitar, mandolin and percussion.

- Mic 2 will be used for an electric guitar amp.

- Mic 3 will be used for vocals.

Starting with Acoustic Guitar

First, we'll lay down an acoustic groove.

Example 4-2

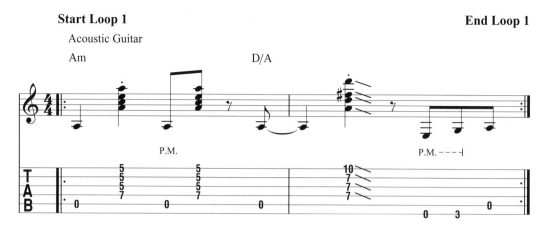

Adding Percussion

Next, we'll record some bongos.

Adding Mandolin

Now let's add a little mandolin.

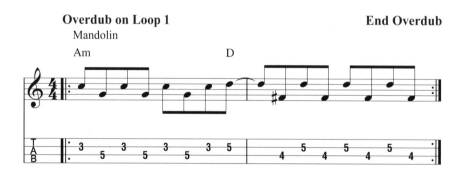

Adding Electric Guitar

How about an electric guitar part? This isn't an acoustic instrument, of course, but we've got a microphone on the amp, which means it's fair game for the Ditto Mic Looper.

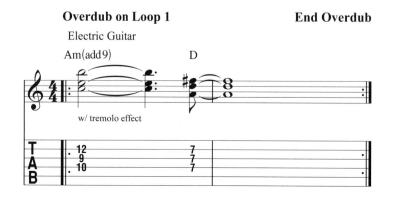

Adding Vocals

And finally, let's add two background vocal parts.

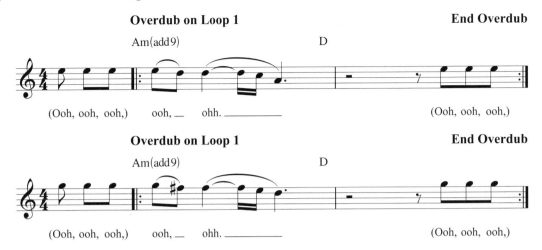

And there we have it: a five-layer loop combining acoustic guitar, percussion, mandolin, electric guitar, and vocals, and we didn't have to adjust a mic once! So as you can see, if you have a few extra mics lying around and a mixer, your options with a mic looper will really open up quite a bit!

Using a Looper with Guitar and Mic Inputs ▶

Another option for incorporating a mic looper is to use a device that has both guitar and mic inputs. There are several possible options on the market, ranging in price from around $300 to $800 and more. Some popular ones include (from low to high in price):

- Digitech JML2 JamMan
- Boss RC-30
- Line 6 JM4
- Boss RC-300
- TC Helicon VoiceLive 3 Extreme

I'll be using a TC Helicon VoiceLive 3 Extreme for these demonstrations. In this example, we'll try combining ukulele, acoustic guitar, electric guitar, a bit of percussion, and vocals. (Note that the VoiceLive 3 Extreme contains a three-track looper, but I'll only be using the first loop for this demonstration.) To make the instrument changing a bit easier, I'll be using a switching device, which I'll explain in a bit.

Gear Spotlight: TC Helicon VoiceLive 3 Extreme

The VoiceLive 3 Extreme is an incredibly powerful unit combining a staggering amount of vocal effects (including a smart harmony generator) and guitar effects (including amp simulation), as well as an incredibly versatile three-track looper (two can be played simultaneously) and full MIDI capability. You can fully automate all the vocal and guitar effects, allowing you to concentrate solely on the performance, and you can augment your sound to your heart's content with the use of backing tracks if you'd like. Or, you can use it simply as a multi-effect stompbox pedal board if you want and run it through your favorite amp. It has enough inputs and outputs to choke a bear, allowing a wide range of setup applications. And though the functionality goes as deep as you'd want to go—it's hard to even summarize the endless possibilities in this unit—the ten onboard color-coded(!) footswitches make operating the unit quick and intuitive once you know the basics.

Although the VoiceLive 3 Extreme would be severe overkill for someone who just wants a looper to practice soloing over a chord progression, it's an ideal tool for the singer-songwriter who wants the ultimate in flexibility for a one-man show. Its power and versatility have few matches out there.

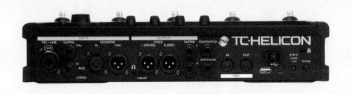

Gear Spotlight: TC Helicon VoiceLive 3 Extreme

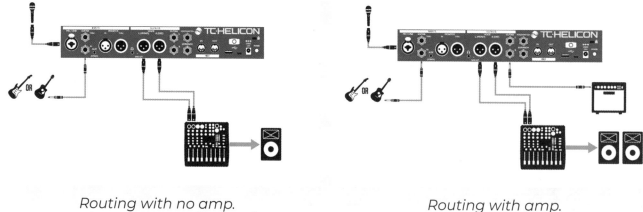

Routing with no amp.   *Routing with amp.*

Starting with Ukulele

First, we'll begin with a ukulele strumming riff. I'm basically just plugging my ukulele into the Voice-Live 3 Extreme (VL3X). (I say "basically" because there's one part of the chain I'm skipping over for the moment, which I'll get to in a bit.) To start recording on the VL3X, we push the HARMONY/DRIVE switch and start playing. To punch out, push the same switch again, which puts us in playback mode. Here's the uke part.

Example 4-3

Adding Acoustic Guitar

Next up, we'll add a little, bass-register riff on the acoustic. This is where the switching device comes into play. I'm using the ABC from Morley (see sidebar) so I don't have to do any unplugging to change instruments. I have the ukulele, acoustic guitar, and electric guitar all plugged into the ABC, and I just push the appropriate footswitches to select the acoustic guitar and deselect the ukulele. In order to overdub on the VL3X, we just push the same HARMONY/DRIVE switch while in playback mode—both for punch in and punch out. And now here's the acoustic part.

Overdub on Loop 1

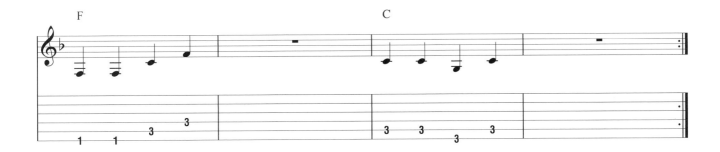

Gear Spotlight: Morley ABC

The ABC from Morley is a switching device that allows you to do one of two things:

- Send one signal to three different places.
- Send three different signals to one place.

It features one In/Out jack and three jacks labeled A, B, and C. In the example listed on the previous page, you could send one guitar, for example, to three different amp rigs or any combination of them. In the second example—which is what I'm doing—you could have three different instruments plugged in and send them all to one rig. Then, you could have any or all of them active.

The ABC features LEDs to show which connections are active and requires 9V power (battery or adapter) for use with the LEDs. However, you can also use it in passive mode with no power. The LEDs won't light, but the connections will still be active. The ABC features a steel enclosure guaranteed to withstand years of use and true-bypass circuitry. It's quite a handy little box around if you plan to do a lot of instrument switching!

Adding Electric Guitar

We'll add a tremolo electric guitar part to our loop next. Now that I've selected the electric guitar with the ABC box, I need to change presets on the VL3X to the appropriate electric sound. I'll be using an amp simulator and a tremolo effect, all of which are coming from the VL3X.

Now let's record the electric part.

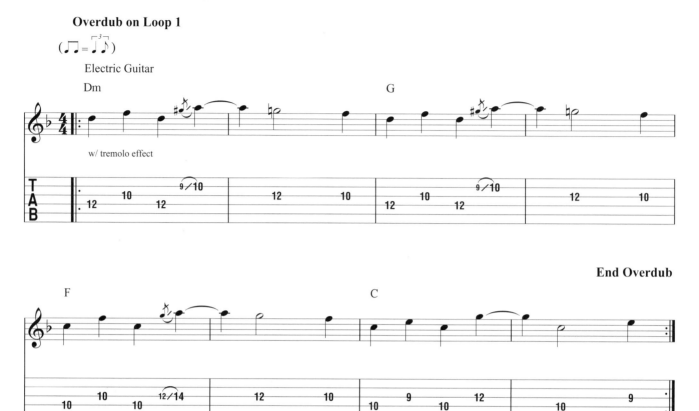

Adding Percussion

Next, we'll add some percussion. First, we'll record a shaker and then some bongos, both using the microphone (which is plugged into the VL3X's mic input). (If you're coordinated enough, you could even do both parts at the same time!) I've added a bit of reverb with the VL3X.

Here's the shaker.

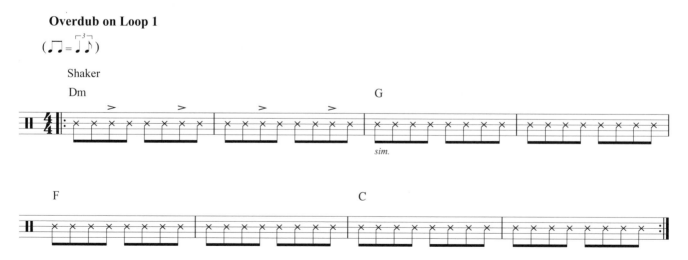

And now here are the bongos.

Adding Vocals

Finally, we'll add vocals to complete the loop. Again, we'll overdub these in one continuous pass, thereby committing them to one layer, which could be undone and redone from section to section. Again, the VL3X is providing some reverb for the vocals.

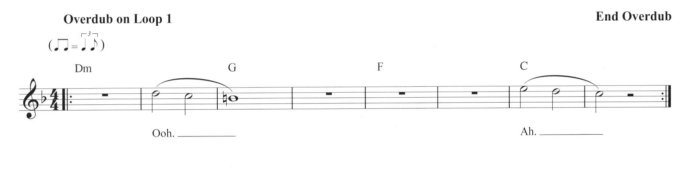

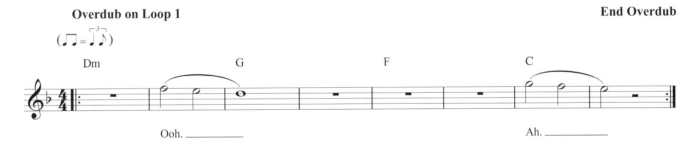

So there are numerous ways to incorporate mic'd instruments or vocals into your loops. If you want to keep it relatively simple, the Ditto Mic Looper may be all you need. But if you want to be able to seamlessly incorporate electric instruments (such as guitar and bass) with acoustic ones (such as vocals, acoustic guitar, percussion, etc.), then you'll most likely want to check out a more full-featured unit that includes both instrument and mic inputs. Granted, pairing the Ditto Mic Looper with a mic mixer allows for a good amount of flexibility, but if you're really wanting an all-in-one solution, it's hard to beat something like the TC Helicon VoiceLive 3 Extreme or Boss RC-300.

Chapter 5: Getting Creative with Effects and Alternate Sound Sources

Thus far, all the loops we've created have consisted of very standard sounds. Aside from some tremolo on an electric guitar in Example 4-3, we haven't used any effects. Where's the fun in that? In this chapter, we're going to look at some ways we can use effects to dress up our loops in creative ways. We'll also look at some alternative sound sources that can be harnessed in interesting ways.

I'll be using the Ditto X4 Looper for these examples, which has its own set of built-in effects, but I'll also be incorporating some other effects, too. You won't likely have all the same pedals I do—or maybe you will; some people really love to hoard pedals!—but there are plenty of options available out there that will usually accomplish a similar task.

Reverse/Backward Effect

We'll start with the *reverse* or *backward* effect. This effect plays your loop in reverse, and it's one of my favorites. Not all loopers feature this effect, but many do. The possibilities with this effect are vast, and it's a shame that many people think of this as nothing but a novelty. We're going to look at two basic categories about using this effect:

- Building a backward soundscape, over which you play/loop normally.

- Building a normal loop, over which you overdub a mixture of forward and backward elements.

Another way of saying this is loops that are intended to be played backwards (the first type) or loops that are intended to be played forward (the second type). Of course, there's no hard and fast line between these two approaches; they just tend to be the basic parameters I consider when using the reverse effect. Many loops you build could contain elements of both these approaches, but it seems to me that many examples will fall within one of these two basic categories.

Building a Backward Soundscape ▶️

In this type of loop, we'll start off overdubbing several layers normally. Then, we'll flip the loop to reverse mode and continue playing and/or looping over the top from there. We want to create a nice bed of backwards sound over which we'll play normally. This loop is designed to ultimately be playing in reverse mode.

Looping Tip!

If you've not messed around with backwards audio much yet, it takes some getting used to. You have to remember that, for example, any chord progression you play will appear in reverse when you flip (reverse) the loop. So if you play Em–C–G–B7, for example, it's going to play as B7–G–C–Em when you flip it. If you're going to be playing some melodies or solos over the backward loop, be sure to keep this in mind!

Let's start out with a bass-register riff that implies a chord progression. What we want to end up with—once the loop is flipped and played backwards—is a progression of Em–C–G–B7. This means we need to reverse those chords for now and play B7–G–C–Em. So our bass riff needs to imply those same chords.

Example 5-1

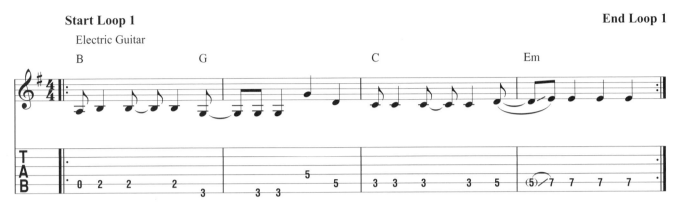

Now let's add a few arpeggios to fill things out a bit.

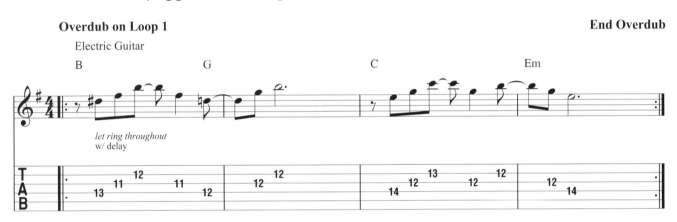

And finally, we'll add some long, sparse dyads to get a nice swelling sound when the loop is flipped.

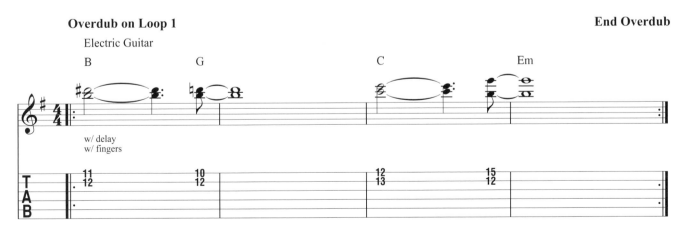

OK, so we've got our nice three-layer loop; time to flip it. On the Ditto X4, we select REVERSE on the FX knob. Wait for the loop to reach the beginning of the cycle and then push the FX switch. Now the loop will play in reverse. (You can push the FX button to flip the loop at any point in the cycle. It just helps to get your bearings a bit if you flip it right at the beginning.) Sit back and check it out, and try to get your bearings as to where beat 1 is.

We now hear the Em–C–G–B7 chord progression we wanted to hear from the beginning, only it sounds backwards. You're now free to solo over the top to your heart's content, or you could add more to the loop. Anything you add now—assuming you don't flip the loop again back to forward—will sound normal atop the backwards soundscape.

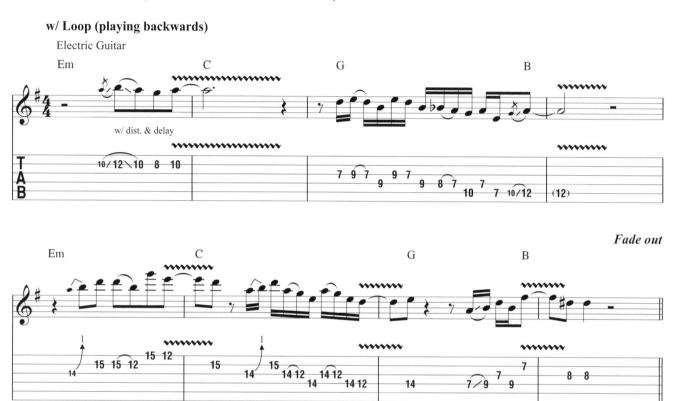

Combining Backward and Forward Elements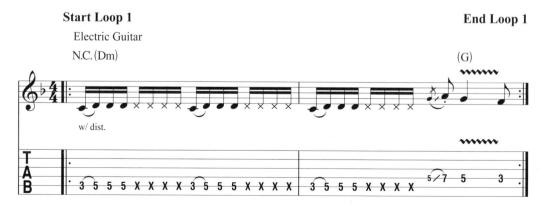

This is another really fun use for the reverse effect, but it can be a little tricky at first. The idea is to create a normal loop; it can be one layer or more. Then, you reverse the loop and record some ideas while the loop is playing backwards. Then, you flip the loop again so that it's playing forwards, but it'll have a mixture of forward and backward sounds. This loop is designed to ultimately be playing in forward (normal) mode.

First, let's lay down a low-end riff in D minor to serve as the backbone.

Example 5-2

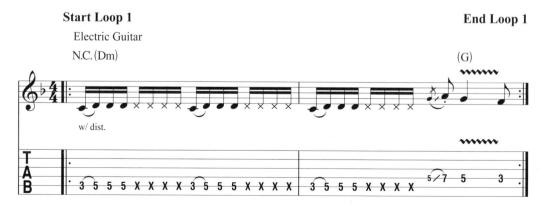

Now we'll add a couple of counter melodies, recorded as one layer.

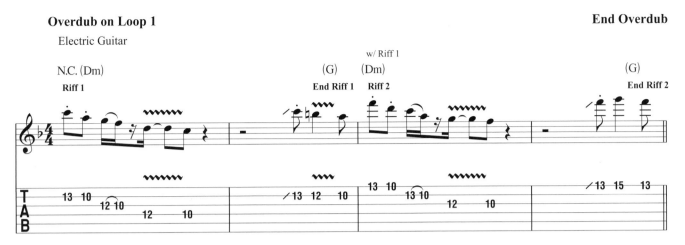

OK, now let's flip the loop and add some harmonized melodies on top. On the Ditto X4, again we have the knob set to REVERSE and then push the FX switch. This is the tricky part, as it can be very hard to hear the beats properly depending on the rhythm of your primary loop. We'll record these two parts again in one pass.

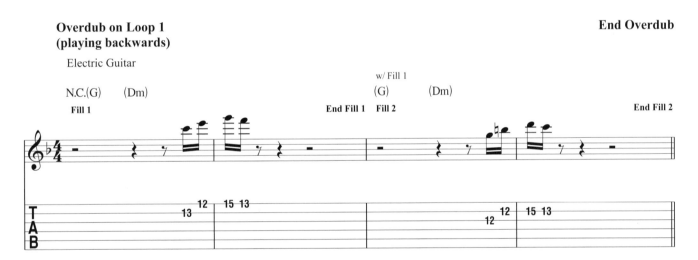

Looping Tip!

Again, remember the backwards rule! If you want to end up with a backwards-sounding melody that ascends in pitch, then you need to record it as a descending melody while the loop is playing backwards and vice versa. Up is down, and down is up!

Turn to the next page to see all of the parts shown in a complete score.

Now flip the loop back again to normal mode (push the FX switch on the Ditto X4) and check out what we have! Here's everything together.

*Backwards guitar.

**Backwards guitar.

Swells and More Swells! ▶️

This is one of my favorite applications for the backwards effect: creating a big, dramatic swell with lots of overdubs. The idea is to have the swell build up to something interesting. This loop is designed to ultimately be played in forward (normal) mode, too.

First, let's start with a descending chord riff that culminates is a high dyad.

Example 5-3

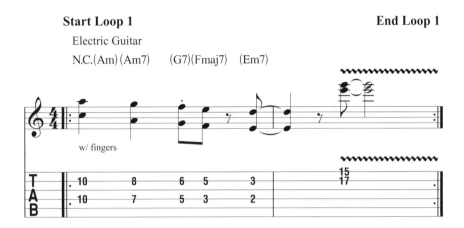

Let's overdub a harmony for that dyad to thicken it up a bit more.

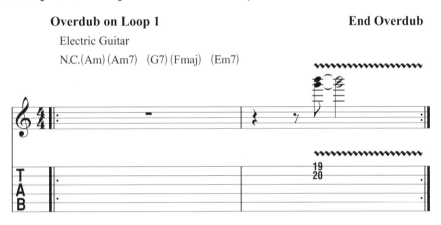

And now let's flip the loop and start overdubbing several parts to create a big swell leading to that dyad. Since we want to accentuate the dyad, we'll play these notes about an eighth note after we hear the dyad disappear. Here's the first overdub.

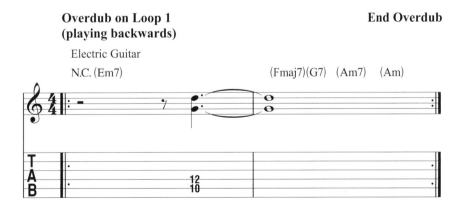

Here's the second.

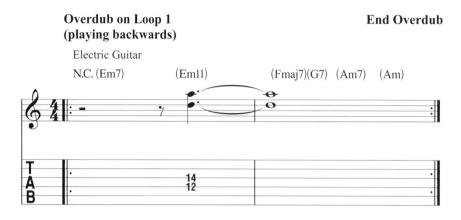

And here's the third.

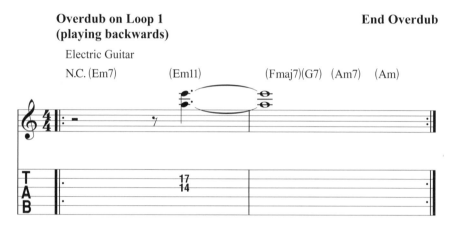

Now let's add one more backward element—a little bass riff—to round it off.

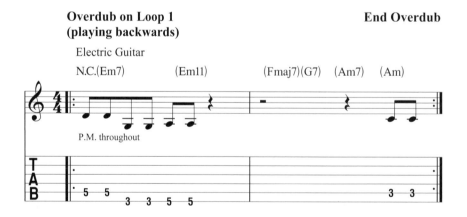

Now let's flip the loop back to forward again and check it out! Here's what we've got. To save paper, I've grouped the overdubs into three different elements: the original loop plus high harmony dyad, the backwards swell dyads, and the backwards bass riff. (This is all located on the next page.)

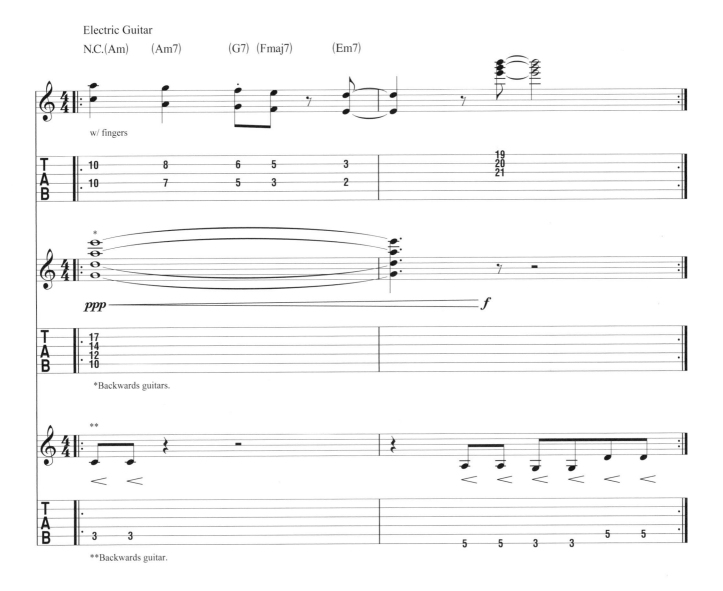

*Backwards guitars.

**Backwards guitar.

Backwards Delay

Another fun effect can be created by using a delay in conjunction with the reverse effect. Let's give that shot. First, we'll lay down a clean-tone riff here as a foundation.

Example 5-4

Now let's turn on a delay and set the feedback so we get several repeats. Next, we'll flip the loop to play it backwards. Then, we'll overdub a staccato part to make the delays nice and audible.

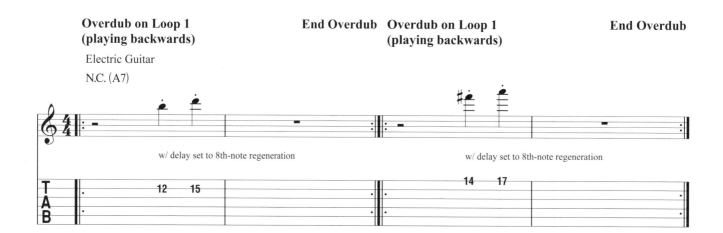

Now flip the loop back again to hear the result. Instead of fading away after the initial attack, the delays get louder! Here's the result. Again, we've consolidated the loop onto two staves to save space.

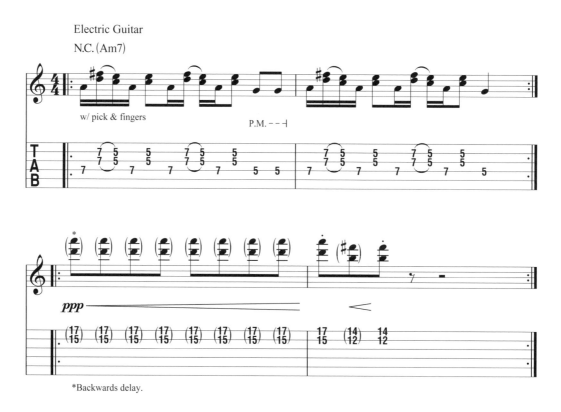

*Backwards delay.

Octaver Effect for Creating Bass Lines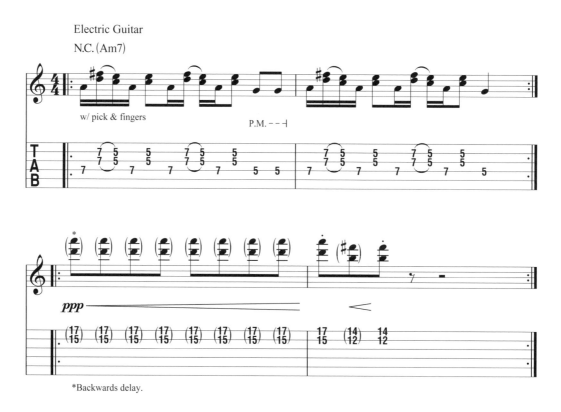

This is another very common effect for "one-man-band" artists. You can use an octaver or pitch transposer effect to play a bassline with your guitar. There are a thousand devices out there that will do this. I'm going to be using a MicroSynth from Electro-Harmonix—an extremely fun pedal that can create countless synth-like tones, not to mention a great bass simulation.

Make sure your looper is at the end of your pedal chain for these examples, as we'll be changing sounds from one layer to the next. First, here's a rhythm guitar part, located on the next page.

Example 5-5

Start Loop 1

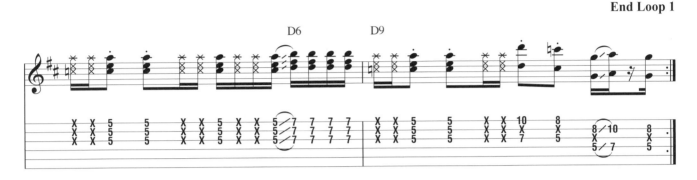

End Loop 1

Next, let's turn the MicroSynth (or octaver of your choice) on and overdub a bass line.

And voila! You've got a full-bodied bass/guitar loop that's ready for solos, vocals, or more overdubs.

Half Speed/Double Speed

These are two other common effects found on several loopers, including the Ditto X4. The half speed effect plays the loop back at half speed (and usually an octave down), while the double speed effect plays the loop twice as fast (and usually an octave up). If you record while in either of these modes, the layer will be affected appropriately when the loop is played back normally.

First, let's try the half speed effect. We'll start with a chord riff here at normal speed.

Example 5-6

Start Loop 1   **End Loop 1**

Now let's move to half speed. On the Ditto X4, we turn the FX knob to HALF and then press the FX footswitch. The loop now plays at half speed and one octave lower. Anything we record now will sound double-speed and one octave up when we return to normal-speed playback. Keep this in mind when choosing your part to play. Let's record two harmony guitar lines. Here's the first one.

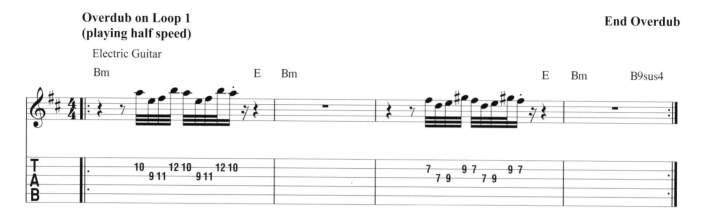

And here's the second.

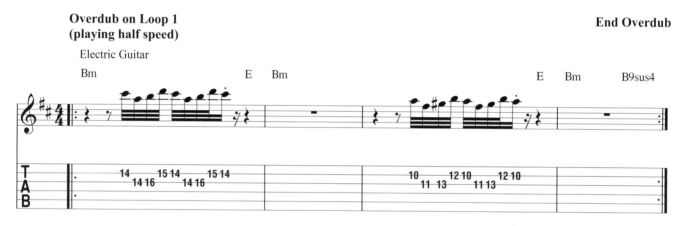

Now let's bring the loop back to normal speed. On the Ditto X4, we just push the FX button again to turn off the half speed effect.

Let's do two more overdubs here, only using the double speed effect this time. On the Ditto X4, turn the FX knob to DOUBLE and push the footswitch again to play the loop at double speed. Everything will sound twice as fast and one octave higher. Anything we record now will sound half-speed and one octave lower when we return to normal-speed playback. Here's the first melody.

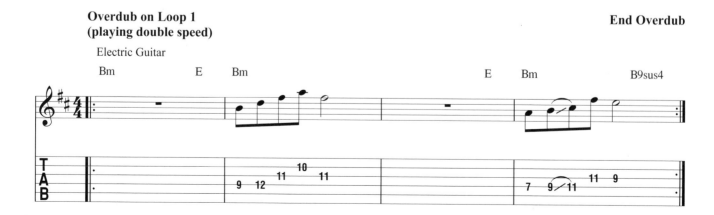

Here's one more.

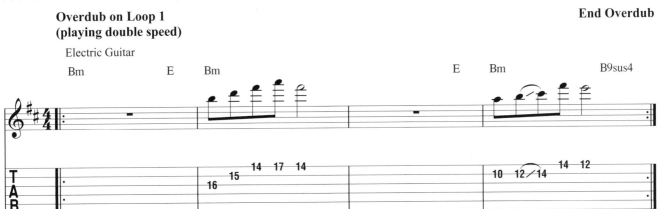

Let's add some final punches on beat 4.

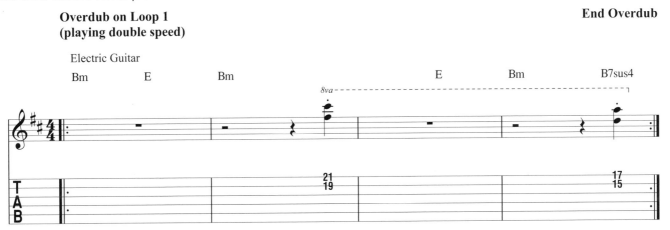

Now let's return to normal speed and have a listen. On the Ditto X4, just push the FX button again to turn off the double speed effect. Fun stuff!

Creating a Bass Line with the Half Speed Effect ▶️

If you don't have an octave pedal, you can still simulate a bass line with your guitar using the half-speed effect on your looper. It just takes a little forethought. Once you have the bass line ready, you need to learn how to play it at double speed, because that's how you'll need to record it.

So let's say we're going to play this bass line, and the goal tempo is around 90 bpm. We need to record it at 180 bpm first, which will sound like this:

Example 5-7

Depending on the complexity of the line, obviously this can take some practice. Many times, double speed is a lot faster than you expect it to be!

Now we'll play the loop back at half speed. Again, on the Ditto X4, we turn the FX knob to HALF and push the FX switch. And presto! We have the bass line we want at the tempo we want.

Alternative Sounds with the Guitar ▶

Who says we have to play the guitar traditionally? You can generate all kinds of interesting sounds with the guitar just by experimenting. Many of these will sound pretty interesting when put into the context of a loop. Here are just a few things to try:

- Tapping the strings at various spots.
- Strumming behind the nut.

- Tapping on the pickups with a screwdriver (or something else metallic).
- Scraping the strings with the pick.

And of course, you could combine any of these sounds with other effects, such as an octaver, delay, reverse, etc.

Let's build a loop now with some various percussive sounds and then layer some more traditional parts on top of it. We'll start by tapping the pick on the deadened B and E strings to simulate a metallic, hi-hat-like sound.

Example 5-8

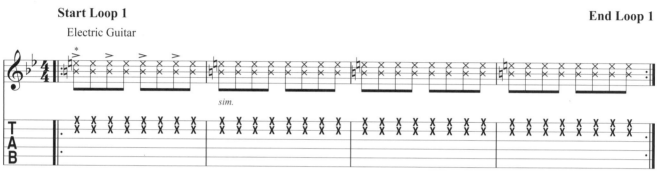

Next, we'll tap the strings in two different spots to loosely simulate a low drum and high drum—kind of a bass/snare effect. For the bass simulation, I'll engage an octaver.

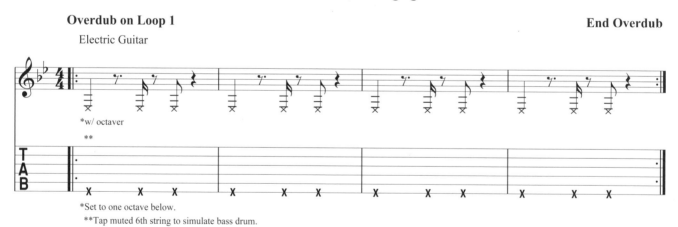

And I'll turn that off for the snare simulation.

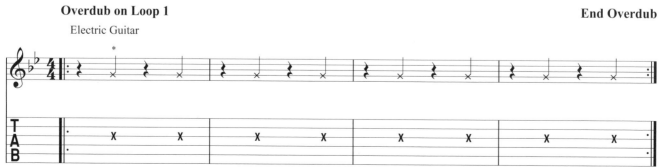

Now we have a nice little electronic percussion loop, over which we can lay a guitar riff.

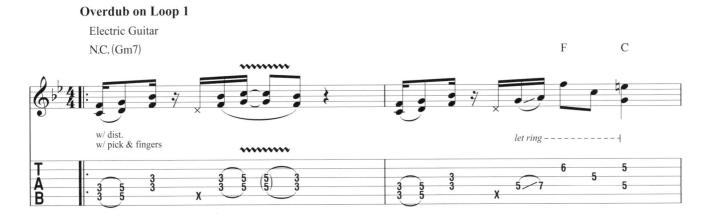

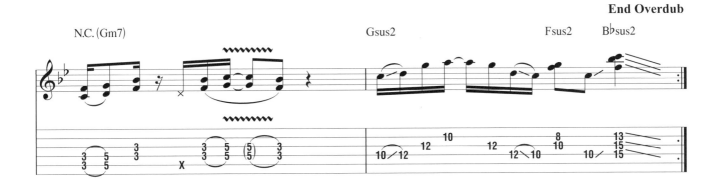

Let's try one more quick one in which we combine some alternative sounds with the reverse effect. Let's start with this tapped rhythm that involves both hands tapping on the strings.

Example 5-9

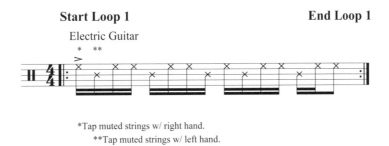

*Tap muted strings w/ right hand.
**Tap muted strings w/ left hand.

Now let's flip the loop, so this part sounds backwards. We'll add some picked dead notes—two parts in one pass.

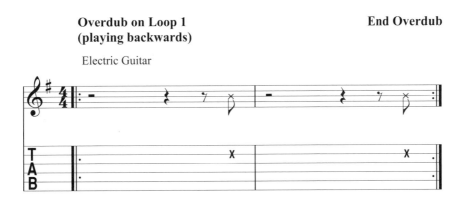

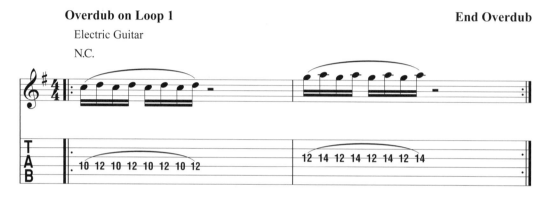

Next, let's add some harmonized hammer-ons and pull-offs. Again, we'll do two parts in one pass.

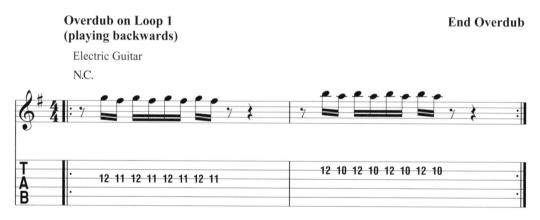

And let's flip the loop again and do another round of little two-note ostinatos. To mix things up, we'll pluck these instead of hammering and pulling again.

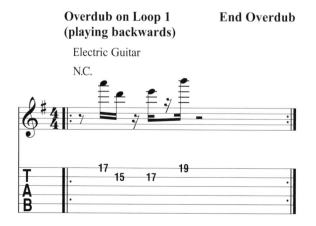

And let's add one higher melody here as icing on the cake.

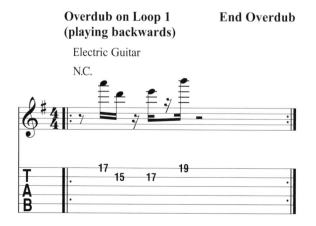

Finally, since the last two parts were meant to sound backwards, let's flip the loop again and check everything out. Here's what we've got. (Again, similar elements have been condensed onto a single staff.)

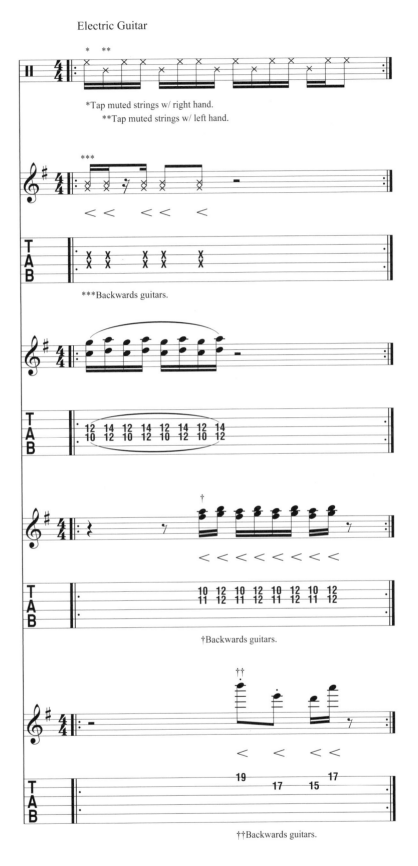

Electric Guitar

*Tap muted strings w/ right hand.
**Tap muted strings w/ left hand.

***Backwards guitars.

†Backwards guitars.

††Backwards guitars.

This is just scratching the surface of possibilities when it comes to effects and alternative sounds, etc. Carve out some time to experiment on your own, and you'll most likely come up with some stuff that you really dig.

Chapter 6: Multi-track Looping Techniques

Just when you think you have a handle on single-loop techniques, now come the multi-track loops! Using more than one loop opens up a world of possibilities in regards to form and loop texture. It's hard to believe sometimes what we can create with a single loop; having access to two (or more) loops widens the aperture even more.

The technique of loop-building on a multi-track looper is basically the same as with a single-loop device, but there are several other factors that come into play with regard to how you want the loops to interact with each other and how you want the looper to respond to your workflow. This makes knowing your particular looper even more important because things can start to get a bit more complicated.

In this chapter, I'll be demonstrating these techniques with the TC Electronic Ditto X4 Looper (two loops) and the TC Helicon VoiceLive 3 Extreme (three loops). Again, be sure to consult your looper's manual to see how it accomplishes these same functions, as it will likely be different from the ones I'm using.

We're going to divide these examples into two broad categories that we'll call *sync mode* and *serial mode*. These are basically two different ways that we can use multiple loops on a multi-track device.

Sync Mode

In sync mode, the two (or more) loops will play simultaneously. This is mostly used for creating variable textures for one repeating section of music. For example, Loop 1 may contain percussion and bass only, while Loop 2 may contain rhythm guitar and some other layers. (Some loopers may refer to multiple loops as Loop A, Loop B, etc.) Maybe you'd use only Loop 1 for the verses of the song and then add Loop 2 for the choruses, etc. This is only one possible scenario; you can of course make use of multiple loops for instrumental tunes as well.

Sync Loop Example 1

So let's set up an example similar to what we just described above. We'll have percussion and bass (simulated with a guitar or using a real bass) on Loop 1 and then we'll add several more sounds on Loop 2. Since we'll be using a mic for the percussion sounds, I'll use the VoiceLive 3 Extreme (VL3X) for this.

First, we need to make sure we're set to record on Loop 1. On the VL3X, this is referred to as Loop A. When I'm ready to record, so I push the HARMONY/DRIVE switch, which is set to REC A (record Loop A). First up is the shaker. So I'll push record and start shaking. Remember to make the loop as long as you need for all the instruments—not just for the shaker part! This loop is going to be two measures long, so I need to set that length right now by recording two measures of shaker.

Example 6-1

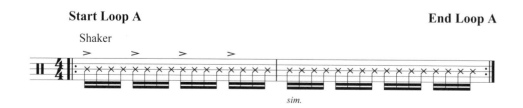

When I'm done with the part, I push the same switch to punch out, and the loop will start playing back. At this point, let's overdub some bongos. The same HARMONY/DRIVE switch is now set to ODUB A (overdub on Loop A), so all we have to do is push it to punch in for the bongos overdub and press it again to punch out.

OK, that takes care of the percussion. Let's add a bassline now. Since the VL3X can accept a bass guitar too, you could plug in an actual bass if you wanted. But we'll simulate it with a guitar by using an octaver effect. After selecting the sound we want to use, we're ready to overdub. Again, we punch in and out with the same HARMONY/DRIVE switch.

Great! Now we've got our Loop A complete with three layers: shaker, bongos, and bass. It's time to move on to Loop B. Before we do this, we need to make sure that we're set to sync mode (and not serial). This is set by default on the VL3X, but check with your looper to see how it functions.

The VL3X defaults to SMART sync mode, which means it will automatically adjust the length of Loop B to the same as Loop A or a multiple of it. In other words, if Loop A is two measures, Loop B can be two measures, four measures, six measures, etc. (This feature can be disabled if you don't want the loops to stay in sync.)

I'll turn off the octaver and select a sound for my rhythm guitar part on the VL3X, and, assuming Loop A is playing back (if it's not, start playback), we're ready to go with our first layer on Loop B. Press the REVERB switch, which is linked to REC B (record on Loop B), to start recording. We press the same switch again to punch out after we're done. Here's the rhythm guitar part.

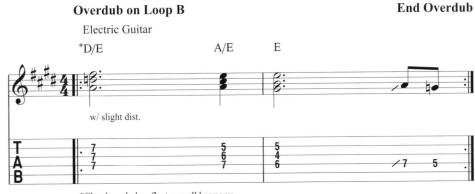

Ditto X4 MODE Switches

When recording a second loop in sync mode, you need to pay attention to when you specifically punch in and out. Since most loopers will default setting the loop at a multiple of the first—i.e., the same length, twice the length, three times the length, etc.—you can end up with more loop than you want if you're not careful.

For example, if you punch in to record on Loop 2 right before the loop cycle begins and then wait until after it ends to punch out, you'll most likely end up with a Loop 2 that lasts twice as long as Loop 1. This is because your "punched in" time was equivalent to more than one cycle of Loop 1. Therefore, the looper will assume that you wanted to create a loop that's longer than Loop 1 and will automatically set the length to be the next multiple of Loop 1 so that everything stays in sync.

This is the default setting for many loopers. Note that, however, many loopers have ways to change this default behavior. The Ditto X4, for example, has four little MODE switches on the back of the unit that can be accessed with a toothpick or pen, etc. The MODE 2 switch changes this behavior in the following way: When set to sync mode, if you push the LOOP 2 switch while LOOP 1 is playing, it will "arm" LOOP 2 for recording (a red LED will flash to indicate this), but it won't start recording until the beginning of the loop cycle. This way, you don't have to worry about punching in a little too early and creating a loop that's twice as long as you wanted. You can punch out at any time, and Loop 2's length will automatically extend to the end of the loop cycle. This means that, if you wait until the loop cycle ends and then punch out, the length of Loop 2 will be twice as long as Loop 1. So you still need to be mindful of when you punch out, but you can be less precise with your punch-in point.

The downside to this is that you're not able to stack up overdubs quite as quickly when working with separate passes because you'll need to wait until the cycle begins again in order to start recording. For example, if you're listening to the loop and decide, "Oh, I want to add one little harmony note there," you won't be able to punch in and out right away to do it. You have to punch in, which will arm the track, and then wait for the cycle to begin again before recording starts.

So as it relates to the Ditto X4, I think the default mode (MODE 2 switch down) is better for more spontaneous creations, whereas the other mode (MODE 2 switch up) is better for more thought-out loops in which you want to ensure precision. The other three MODE switches offer similar variations to the workflow of the pedal.

Notice the "Loop B" indication in the music. Let's add a couple of lead overdubs here as well. We'll record these all in one pass so they can be undone later as a single layer. Here are both parts.

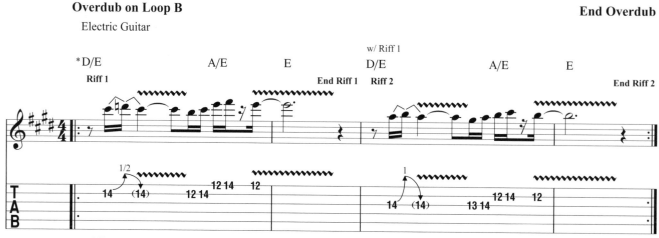

*Chord symbols reflect overall harmony.

So now we have the following six-part phrase divided into two separate loops:

Loop A

- Shaker
- Bongo
- Bass

Loop B

- Rhythm Guitar
- Lead Melody 1
- Lead Melody 2

We can now playback either Loop A, Loop B, or both simultaneously, allowing for a variety of textures. And, since the last thing we recorded was the lead overdubs on Loop B, we can undo them if we want to take a lead break, for example. To do this, we press UNDO, which is mapped to the "Hold for Looper" switch. Then, we can bring them back if we want with REDO, which is mapped to the same switch.

Sync Loop Example 2

Let's do another example, this time using the Ditto X4. For this phrase, we'll use all electric guitar sounds and will make Loop 2 twice as long as Loop 1. On the Ditto X4, we need to set the mini-toggle switch between the LOOP 1 and LOOP 2 knobs to SYNC. This puts us in sync mode, meaning that the loops will play simultaneously.

To start recording on Loop 1, we just push the LOOP 1 switch. Then, we push it again to stop recording and start playing back. We're going to build up a progression in three-part harmony with one note at a time. I'm going to be using my Electro-Harmonix MicroSynth to get a different tone, but this would still sound nice even with a standard guitar tone. Here's the first part.

Example 6-2

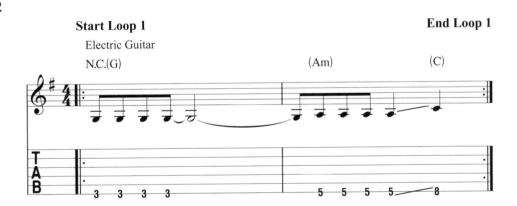

And now we'll overdub the second part. We just put the same LOOP 1 switch to punch in and out.

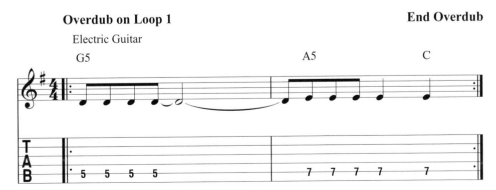

And we repeat the process one more time for the third part.

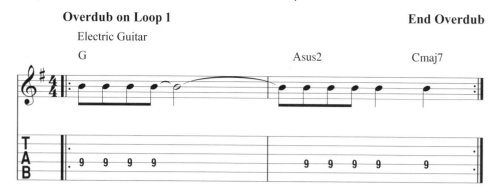

So that completes Loop 1: a nice, mellow chord progression that we could play or sing over for a good while. Now it's time for Loop 2. We'll add some harmonized melody overdubs here with a different sound. I'm going to be using the MicroSynth again, along with a delay.

Once Loop 1 is playing, we just press the LOOP 2 switch on the Ditto X4 to start recording on Loop 2 and press it again to stop recording. Here's the first part.

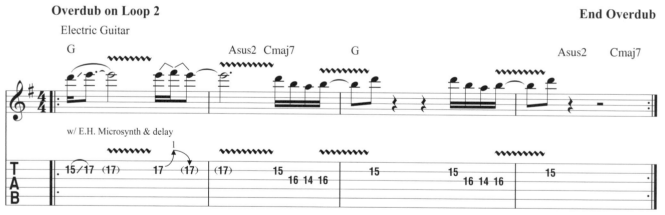

For the second part, it's the same process: LOOP 2 switch to punch in and again to punch out.

And here's the third part.

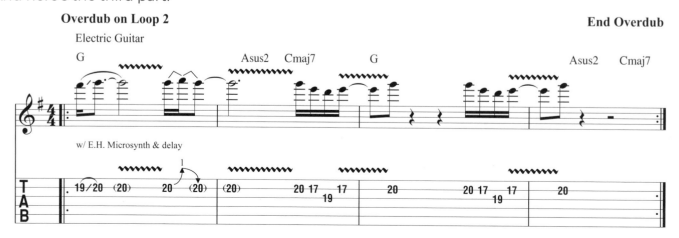

Again, we can play both loops or either one separately to achieve a variety of textures. And don't forget that you can also use UNDO and/or REDO for either loop to achieve even more variation.

Serial Mode

In serial mode, only one loop can play back at a time. This is most commonly used when you want to have different loops set up for different sections of a song. For example, you may build up Loop 1 for the verse and then build up Loop 2 for the chorus, etc. Each loop can be as simple or complex as you'd like, but only one will play at a time. Most loopers make this very easy to do, requiring very little tap-dancing at all. Again, though, you'll most likely need to consult your manual to find out exactly how it works with your looper.

Serial Mode Example 1 ▶️

To quickly show how this is done, we'll make this first example very simple using the Ditto X4. We'll record one chord progression as Loop 1, a second as Loop 2, and then we'll be able to solo over them while they're playing back. This can all be done without missing a beat.

So this will be the sequence of events:

1. Start recording Loop 1.

2. Stop recording Loop 1 and start recording Loop 2.

3. Stop recording Loop 2 and start playing back Loop 1.

4. Solo over Loop 1 or Loop 2 at will.

Here's how it's done on the Ditto X4. First, we make sure the mini-toggle switch between the LOOP 1 and LOOP 2 knobs is set to SERIAL. (Make sure all MODE switches on the back are in their default down position.) When we're ready to start recording chord progression A, we press the LOOP 1 switch and start playing.

Example 6-3

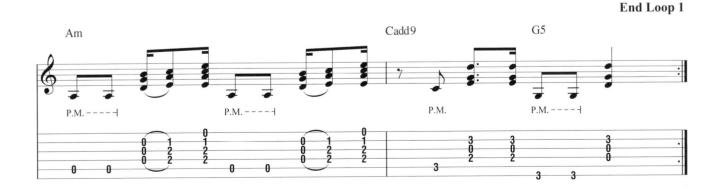

When we reach the end of chord progression A and are ready to start progression B, we just press the LOOP 2 switch. This will stop recording on Loop 1 and start recording on Loop 2 all at the same time. So we press the LOOP 2 switch and keep on playing with the new progression.

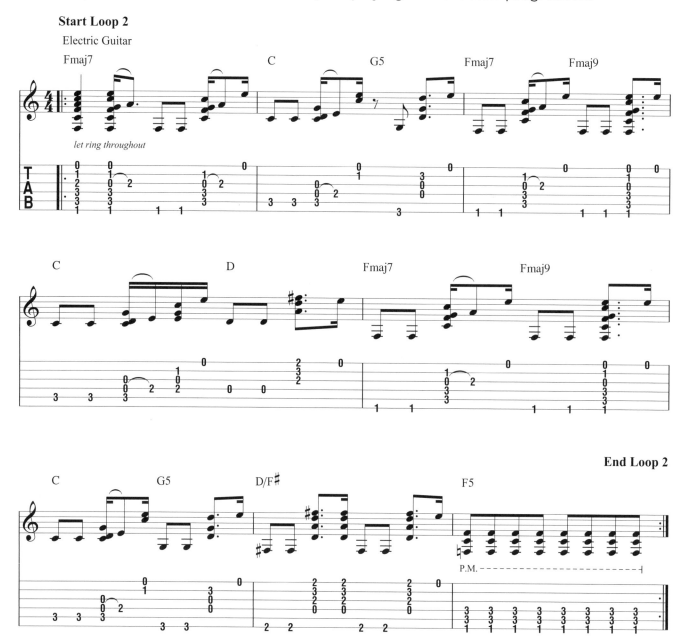

When we reach the end of chord progression B, we have two choices. We can either press the LOOP 1 switch or LOOP 2 switch. Pressing either one will stop recording and start playing back that loop. So we'll press the LOOP 1 switch, which will stop recording Loop 2 and start playing back Loop 1. Then, we can start soloing over Loop 1. If we press the LOOP 2 switch during Loop 1's cycle, it will "cue" Loop 2 to begin playing back after Loop 1 is finished.

Note that, in serial mode on the Ditto X4, Loops 1 and 2 can be completely different lengths and do not have to be multiples of each other. This is likely the way most loopers behave in default mode, but if yours does not, consult your manual.

Serial Mode Example 2 ▶

So now that we've seen a quick example in serial mode, let's create a more fleshed out one, in which both loops are more complex with several layers. With this type of thing, since we're going to be building two loops from the ground up, efficiency is a bit more important because we don't want the audience to get bored. (Of course, if adding witty banter is part of your live show, this may not be as much of a concern, but for those that just want to play, it could be more important.)

To help achieve this, I'm going to set the MODE 1 switch on the back of the Ditto X4 to the up position. This changes the looper's behavior with regard to the order of operations. Normally, when recording the first loop, you press the LOOP 1 switch to start recording and press it again to stop recording and enter playback mode. With the MODE 1 switch up, though, the Ditto X4 will immediately enter overdub mode instead of playback mode. So, the sequence will be:

- Press LOOP 1 switch to enter recording mode.

- Press LOOP 1 switch to stop recording loop and enter overdub mode.

- When finished overdubbing, press LOOP 1 switch to enter playback mode.

So this basically saves you one loop cycle. In other words, you can get an overdub done immediately after setting the length of the loop. After you punch out from the overdub, it behaves the same way as before. Of course, if you don't punch out while overdubbing, you can continue to stack overdubs with each new loop cycle. But again, if you then press UNDO, it will undo all those layers that were recorded during that same extended, multi-cycle overdub.

For this example, I'm going to record the initial loop and the first overdub immediately. Then, I'll punch out and punch back in to record one more overdub before moving on to Loop 2. By doing it this way, I allow for the undoing of the first overdub layer if I make a mistake.

So here we go with the first loop and first overdub. I'll press LOOP 1 to start recording and then press it again when the loop is over. This will establish the loop length and then immediately start overdubbing, so I need to be ready with the first overdub right away. After the first overdub, I'll press LOOP 1 to punch out and enter playback mode.

Example 6-4

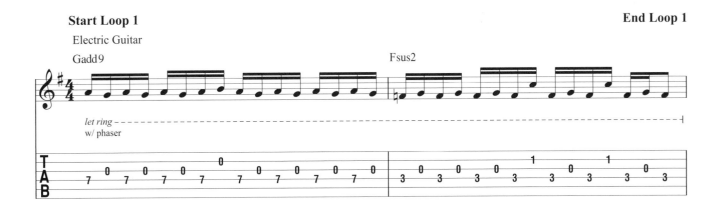

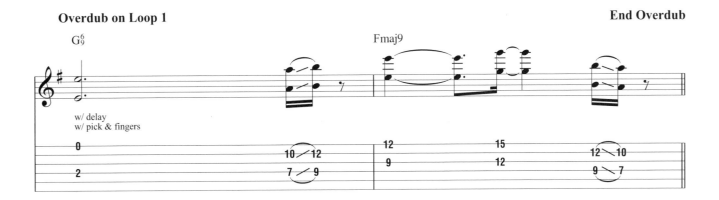

OK, now let's add one more overdub to Loop 1. To do this, we just push the LOOP 1 switch to punch in and then press it again to punch out.

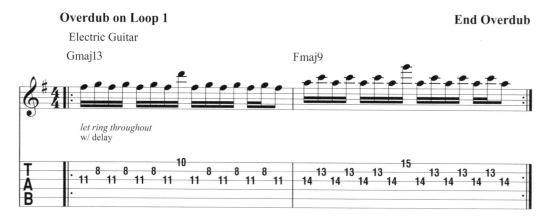

So we have a three-layer loop on Loop 1; now we're going to switch to Loop 2. To start recording Loop 2 on the Ditto X4, we just push the LOOP 2 switch while Loop 1 is playing. This will arm Loop 2, and it will start recording when Loop 1's cycle ends. So we'll do the same process with Loop 2: record the initial loop and first overdub all in one pass. So we press the LOOP 2 switch to start recording, press it again to overdub the first layer, and then press it again to enter playback mode.

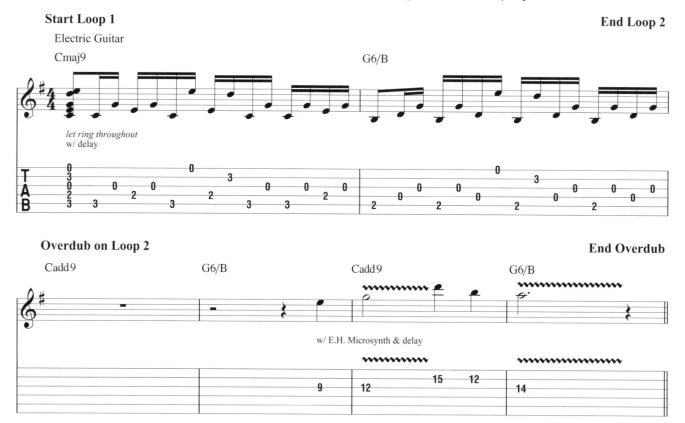

And now let's overdub one more part on Loop 2.

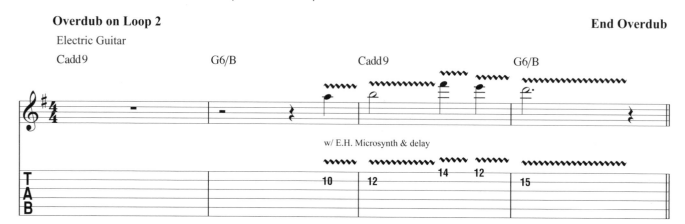

So we end up with two full-sounding loops that we can switch back and forth, either for playing/ singing atop or for building more layers.

More than Two Loops?

Some loopers contain more than two loop tracks. The TC Helicon VoiceLive 3 Extreme, for example, has a three-track looper, but only two can play simultaneously (in sync mode). So you could play back the following:

- Loop A + Loop B

- Loop A + Loop C

- Loop A only

- Loop B only

- Loop C only

Other loopers, such as the 45000 from Electro-Harmonix, can play back as many as four loops simultaneously. Essentially, though, they all boil down to using them in one of these two methods: sync mode or serial mode. In other words, either you're designing the separate loops to be played together or separately.

Chapter 7: Full Loop Performance

We'll close out the book with a full loop performance that ties together almost everything we've learned. We'll use multiple loops, overdubs, effects, UNDO/REDO, and more.

Uphill

This song is an instrumental and will be performed all on electric guitar. I'll use the TC Electronic Ditto X4 Looper for this one, set up two different loops, and even use the backward effect.

Let's start by creating two loops with hand percussion.

Now that we've created a base on which we can layer our overdubs, let's switch over to Loop 1 and lay down a simple, three-note riff.

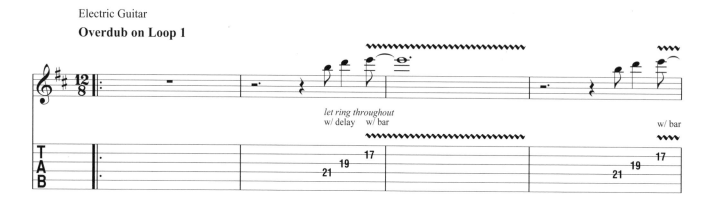

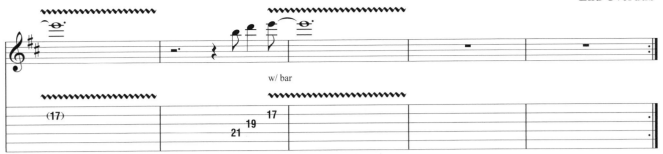

Great! We're ready to layer in some more chords that create a nice call-and-response effect against the riff we previously recorded.

Now that the harmonies are in place, let's overdub some bending figures that ornament the loop, giving us a counter melody to grab onto.

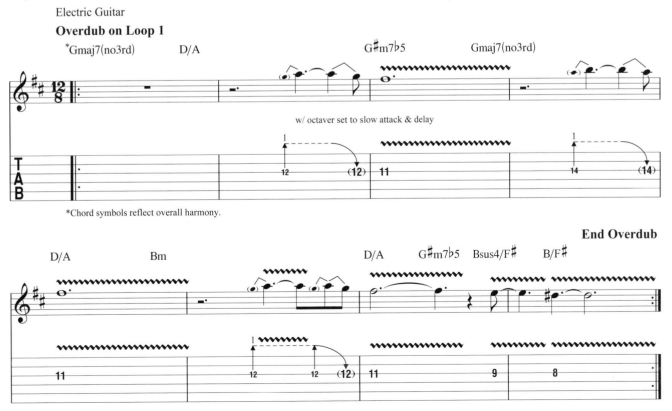

Next, we'll harmonize those bends, approaching from higher pitches.

Now we're ready to add some cool reverse-effect parts. Be sure to keep time and not let the reversed percussion turn you around!

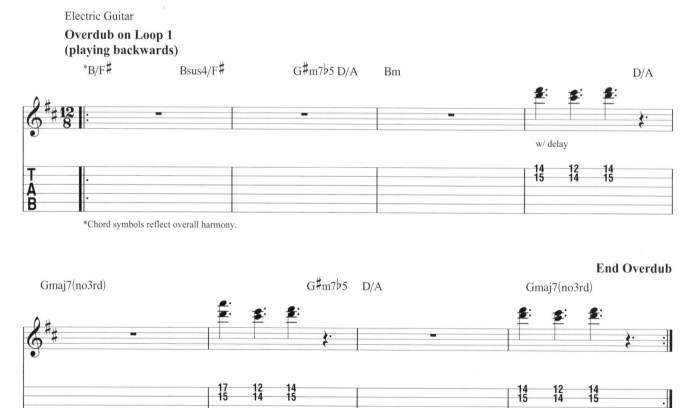

Switch to normal playback, and you have Loop 1 ready to go!

Let's move onto Loop 2. (Don't erase Loop 1; we'll be coming back to it!) At this point, we're switching keys, but we'll layer in similar figures that we played on Loop 1. First, here's the three-note riff, but it's moved around on the fretboard.

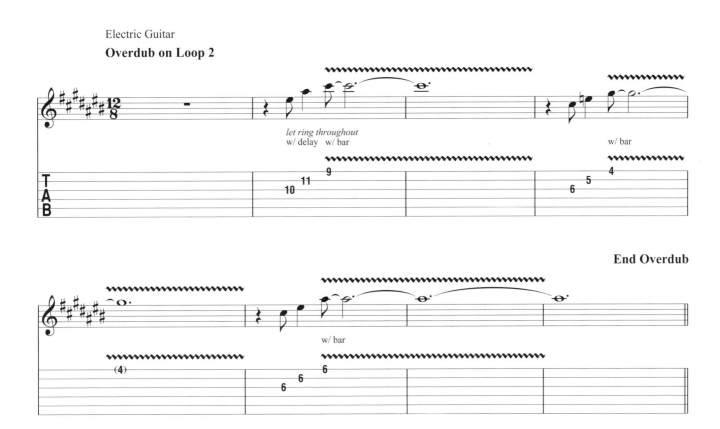

Next, overdub the chords.

Now you're ready for the bending figures.

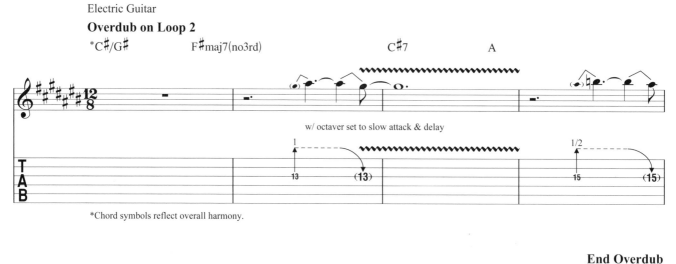

Then, overdub the upper harmony bends.

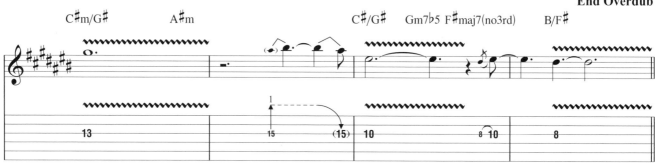

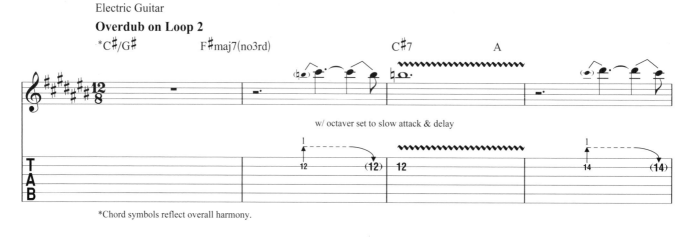

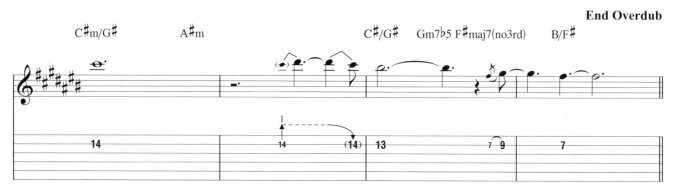

That's it! (For Loop 2, we won't overdub any reverse-effect layers.) Now that you have two loops going, you can choose either of them over which you can improvise or even layer more parts. On the video, I switch back to Loop 1, hit UNDO to remove the reverse effect, and improvise a solo to close out the performance. See what you can do to make it your own!